TENERIFE TRAVEL

Island Escapades: Exploring Tenerife's Natural Beauty and Cultural Delights with Perfect Itinerary for Beginners.

Patsy J. Tour

Copyright ©2023 by Patsy J. Tour

All rights reserved. No part of this publication may be reproduced, distributed, or transmitted in any form or by any means, including photocopying, recording, or other electronic or mechanical methods, without the prior written permission of the copyright holder, except in the case of brief quotations embodied in critical reviews and certain other noncommercial uses permitted by copyright law.

TABLE OF CONTENTS

INTRODUCTION. 9
- WELCOME TO TENERIFE 12
- TENERIFE'S GEOGRAPHY AND CLIMATE: 14
- TENERIFE'S CULTURE AND LANGUAGE: 16
- 11 INTERESTING REASONS WHY YOU SHOULD VISIT TENERIFE 19
- TOP 10 THINGS TO KNOW BEFORE VISITING TENERIFE: 22
- THE DOS AND DON'TS IN TENERIFE 23

CHAPTER 2: ESSENTIAL TRAVEL INFORMATION 27
- 10 SIMPLE STEPS TO PLANNING YOUR NEXT TRIP 27
  - Tips for avoiding the crowds in Tenerife: 29
- EXPENSES AND BUDGETING FOR TENERIFE 29
  - Tenerife Accommodation Budget Average Daily Costs. 30
  - Tenerife Transportation Budget Average Daily Costs. ..31
  - Tenerife Food Budget Average Daily Costs. 31
  - The Cheapest Time to Visit Tenerife 31
  - Tenerife Entertainment Budget Average Daily Costs ...33
  - Tenerife Alcohol Budget Average Daily Costs 33
- HOW TO GET TO TENERIFE 34
- PROS AND CONS OF GETTING TO TENERIFE BY PLANE OR BY FERRY 36
- HOW TO GET AROUND IN TENERIFE 38
  - Tips for Getting around in Tenerife: 39
  - Some pros and cons of each Means of Going Around 40
- THE BEST TIME TO VISIT TENERIFE 42
  - Least crowded times to visit Tenerife: 43
  - Money-saving Tips for your Vacation to Tenerife: 44
- VISA REQUIREMENTS TO TENERIFE....................................46

CHAPTER 3: WHERE TO STAY IN TENERIFE.................49

Accommodation Options in Tenerife 49
Things to consider before booking Accommodation
Tenerife 52
Luxury Hotels and Resorts in Tenerife 56
Mid-Range Hotels and Resorts in Tenerife 57
Budget friendly Hotels and Resorts in Tenerife 58
Best Areas to Stay in Tenerife 59
Some Neighborhoods to Avoid in Tenerife 61
Tips for Avoiding Trouble in Tenerife: 62
Tenerife 3-Day Itinerary: 63
Tenerife Itinerary for 7 Days: 65

CHAPTER 4: FOOD, DINNING AND NIGHT LIFE 70

Canarian Traditional Dishes 70
Well-known Restaurants and Cafés 73
Local Markets and Street Food 75
Dietary Restrictions and Special Requirements 78
Nightclubs and Bars 81
Venues for Music and Entertainment: 83
Performances and Live Music 84
Festivals & Events of Cultural Interest: 86
Gaming and Casinos 87

CHAPTER 5: PRACTICAL INFORMATION 90

Safety and Travel Tips 90
Considerations for Health and Safety 90
Customs and Local Laws 92
Emergency Phone Numbers. 95
Medical Services and Travel Insurance. 97
Money and Tipping. 100
Useful Phrases and Vocabulary 104
Basic Greetings and Expressions 104
Numbers and Directions 107
Dining and Shopping Phrases 110

CHAPTER 6: EXPLORING TENERIFE. 113
15 Things to do and See in Tenerife 113
Tips for Solo Travelers to Tenerife 119
Tips for Female Solo Travelers to Tenerife 120
Tips for Family Travelers to Tenerife........................122
Top Booking Resources:..123

CONCLUSION 125

INTRODUCTION.

I began a voyage that would live on in my mind for the rest of my life. It was an expedition to Tenerife, a destination of stunning scenery, lively culture, and great hospitality. I had no idea that I was about to embark on an incredible adventure when I stepped foot on this Spanish jewel. My first day started with the sun shining brightly down on the beautiful shoreline. I was captivated to the beautiful beaches that surrounded the island. I felt revitalized and eager to explore the island's beauties after a refreshing plunge in the crystal-clear waters of Playa de las Teresitas. Curiosity drove me towards the center of the island, where nature displayed its splendor. The breathtaking grandeur of the famed Teide National Park lured me. I joyfully approached the slopes of Mount Teide, Spain's highest summit and a dormant volcano. As I neared the top, I was met with a bizarre scene: a sea of clouds extending underneath me, with nearby islands seeming as tiny specks on the horizon. The sheer beauty of the environment took my breath away, and I couldn't help but record the moment on film, knowing that the experience would be treasured for the rest of my life.

As I continued my investigation, I came upon the charming settlement of Masca, which was tucked among rocky cliffs. Its twisting, narrow alleyways took me through a maze of whitewashed buildings covered with vivid blossoms. Following that was a hike into the stunning Masca Gorge, where towering rock formations and lush flora enveloped me. The suspense rose with each step, and at the end of the route, I was rewarded with a view of a hidden cove and the soothing caress of the Atlantic Ocean's waves. The peace of the surroundings enveloped my spirit, leaving an unforgettable imprint on my heart. Tenerife's attractiveness extended beyond its natural beauty. The colorful culture of the island attracted me at every step. I experienced the grandeur of the yearly Carnival in Santa Cruz de Tenerife, a bright festival that filled the streets with music, dancing, and vivid costumes. As residents and tourists alike soaked in the jubilant celebration, the rhythmic beats of drums echoed through the air. I joined the vibrant parade, dancing to the catchy rhythms, and felt a feeling of belonging to the people of the island. It was a celebration of life and an awakening of my soul.

No trip to Tenerife would be complete without sampling the island's exquisite food. I ate traditional Canarian foods that piqued my interest. Mojo sauce tastes accompanied every meal, and fresh fish meals like wrinkled potatoes with mojo verde became my latest addiction. The neighboring vineyards provided a taste of Tenerife's rich wine culture, and I relished the opportunity to enjoy a glass of delicious Malvasia wine as the sun sank over the horizon.

In pursuit of peace, I discovered it in the quiet Anaga Rural Park, where lush trees and craggy mountains coexisted peacefully. The enthralling paths took me through enchanting laurel woods, revealing secret waterfalls and panoramic views. It was a contemplative experience that linked me to the raw beauty of the island, as if nature whispered secrets of calm and tranquility into my ears.

As my stay in Tenerife came to an end, I pondered on the many adventures that had enhanced my vacation. The island had left an unforgettable impact on my spirit, from the breathtaking vistas to the vivid cultural events. It was a location where adventure and tranquillity blended perfectly, and where every moment was a monument to the treasures that await those who dare to explore.

Tenerife had taught me the genuine meaning of travel—immersion in the world's beauty and connection with the people and places that define our lives. I said my goodbyes to this enchanted island, leaving with me memories that would long remind me of the enchantment I had seen. And when I boarded the aircraft, my heart was overjoyed, knowing that Tenerife had given me a memorable chapter in my voyage of discovery.

CHAPTER 1

Welcome to Tenerife

Tenerife is a beautiful island in the Canary Islands archipelago, which is part of Spain. It is the Canaries' biggest and most populated island, drawing millions of people each year with its unique natural beauty, lively culture, and agreeable temperature. Tenerife is located off the northwest coast of Africa and has a subtropical environment that gives pleasant temperatures all year. The island is known for its stunning sceneries, which include golden beaches, towering cliffs, green woods, and volcanic topography.

Mount Teide, Spain's tallest mountain, towers at an astonishing 3,718 meters (12,198 feet) above sea level and is one of the island's most recognizable characteristics. Teide National Park, which surrounds the volcano, is a UNESCO World Heritage site that allows tourists to explore its distinctive volcanic formations, lunar landscapes, and panoramic perspectives.

Tenerife has a rich cultural past that incorporates Spanish, Latin American, and indigenous Guanche influences, in addition to its natural beauty. Santa Cruz de Tenerife, the island's capital, has a mix of modern and old structures, notably the landmark Auditorio de Tenerife, a contemporary performance theater created by renowned architect Santiago Calatrava.

Tenerife is also well-known for its lively festivals and events. The Carnival of Santa Cruz de Tenerife is one of the world's biggest and most magnificent carnival festivities, drawing participants and spectators from all over the world. The city comes alive with bright parades, brilliant costumes, music, and dancing during this exciting celebration. The island has a diverse assortment of activities and attractions to appeal to tourists of all interests. Hiking, mountain biking, surfing, and diving are all popular outdoor activities for adventure seekers. The coastal parts of Tenerife are lined with lovely beaches, such as Playa de las Teresitas, Playa de las Américas, and Playa del Duque, where tourists may rest, swim, and soak up the sun.

Tenerife's food has a delectable selection of traditional Canarian delicacies. Local specialities include arrugadas (wrinkled potatoes) with mojo sauce, fresh fish, and substantial stews. The rich volcanic soil of the island also contributes to the creation of distinctive wines, particularly the Malvasia grape variety. Tenerife's friendly people, contemporary infrastructure, and availability of lodging choices appeal to a wide spectrum of visitors, from budget-conscious backpackers to luxury-seeking tourists. Costa Adeje, Los Cristianos, Puerto de la Cruz, and the aforementioned Santa Cruz de Tenerife are all popular tourist destinations.

Tenerife guarantees an amazing experience for first-time tourists and seasoned travelers alike, whether it's exploring the awe-inspiring natural vistas, immersing oneself in local culture and festivities, or just soaking in the island's year-round sunlight.

Tenerife's Geography and Climate:

Tenerife, the biggest of the Canary Islands, is situated in the Atlantic Ocean, off Africa's northwest coast. It is located at around 28 degrees north latitude and 16 degrees west longitude. The island's topography is varied and intriguing, with a range of vistas to explore. Tenerife's volcanic origin is one of its distinguishing traits. The island was constructed millions of years ago by volcanic activity. Mount Teide is the highlight of Tenerife's geology, a dormant volcano and Spain's tallest mountain, reaching a remarkable height of 3,718 meters (12,198 ft). Teide National Park, which includes Teide and its surrounding regions, is a UNESCO World Heritage site that highlights amazing volcanic structures such as calderas, lava flows, and unusual rock formations.

Tenerife's terrain is varied and distinguished by several areas. The northern half of the island is recognized for its lush vegetation and gorgeous valleys, such as the Orotava Valley, which is well-known for its beautiful botanical gardens. The southern region, on the other hand, has dry landscapes and wonderful coastline locations, with major tourist spots such as Los Cristianos and Playa de las Américas.

Tenerife's coastal districts are home to several stunning beaches. The island accommodates to a variety of beach choices, from beautiful sandy stretches to craggy cliffs and quiet coves. Playa de las Teresitas, located in the northeast, is a beautiful beach with golden sand imported from the Sahara Desert that stands out against the surrounding mountains. Tenerife has a subtropical climate because of its near proximity to the equator. This results in pleasant and temperate temperatures all year. The island has pleasant summers and moderate winters, making it suitable to those looking for a year-round vacation spot.

The cooling impact of the Atlantic Ocean benefits coastal locations, while greater elevations might result in somewhat colder temperatures in the interior. The yearly temperature fluctuates between 20 and 25 degrees Celsius (68 and 77 degrees Fahrenheit).

Tenerife also has an outstanding amount of sunlight hours, which allows for plenty of outdoor activities and sun-soaked leisure.

Tenerife has a varied variety of ecosystems due to its various geology and microclimates, ranging from subtropical woods and lush valleys to desert-like landscapes and volcanic structures. Nature aficionados, hikers, and outdoor explorers will have a one-of-a-kind opportunity to experience the island's rich biodiversity and magnificent natural beauty.

The topography of Tenerife is molded by volcanic origins, with majestic mountain peaks, rich valleys, and attractive seaside places. The island's diversified landscapes and natural attractions, together with its mild subtropical temperature, provide for a wonderful vacation experience.

Tenerife's Culture and Languages

As part of Spain and the Canary Islands, Tenerife has a distinct and lively culture that combines Spanish influences with the island's own particular background. Tenerife's Tinerfeos take great pleasure in their cultural traditions, which are expressed in their language, music, dancing, and food. Tenerife's official language is

Spanish, which is widely spoken across the island. However, owing to the city's reputation as a tourist destination, English is widely spoken, particularly in tourist districts, hotels, and restaurants. Many residents appreciate and embrace tourists' attempts to learn simple Spanish words, which may improve relationships and show respect for the local culture.

Tenerife's cultural legacy is heavily anchored in the island's historical ties to Spain and the indigenous Guanche people. The Guanches were the first residents of the Canary Islands, and their legacy may be seen in traditional crafts, mythology, and place names in Tenerife. Music and dance are important components of Tenerife's cultural expression. Traditional Canarian folk music, known as msica folklórica, has vibrant rhythms, lyrical songs, and unique instruments like the timple (a tiny stringed instrument) and the tamboril (a sort of drum). Folk dances such as the Isa and the Baile de Cintas reflect the island's upbeat and energetic attitude.

Religious festivals and festivities have a distinct position in Tenerife's cultural calendar. One of the most notable events is the Carnival of Santa Cruz de Tenerife, which is regarded as one of the world's biggest and most vivid carnival festivities. The island comes alive at this time with bright parades, lavish costumes, music, and dancing, creating an atmosphere of pleasure and festivity.

Tenerife's culinary culture reflects the island's ethnic variety. Traditional Canarian food blends indigenous products with Spanish influences to create a rich and savory gastronomy. Seafood plays an important part, with popular meals including fresh fish, octopus, and limpets (known as lapas). Tenerife is also noted for its usage of mojo sauces, which are spicy condiments created from components like as garlic, peppers, and spices. The rich volcanic soil of the island allows the development of fruits such as bananas, mangoes, and avocados, which are used in a variety of cuisines and sweets.

Tenerife's cultural heritage include art and craftwork. Pottery, woodwork, basket weaving, and needlework are just a few of the crafts created by skilled artists. These traditional crafts not only highlight the residents' ability and ingenuity, but they also serve as a means to conserve and pass down cultural legacy from generation to generation. Tenerife visitors may immerse themselves in the island's rich culture by attending festivals, visiting museums and cultural institutions, and touring traditional communities. The Tinerfeos' warmth and friendliness add to the cultural experience, as they enjoy sharing their traditions, tales, and local customs with guests.

Tenerife's culture is a compelling combination of Spanish and Guanche elements, shown in language, music, dance, food, and crafts. Exploring the island's cultural offerings gives a greater knowledge and respect of the native way of life, leaving those who are lucky enough to experience this unique cultural tapestry with lasting memories and relationships.

11 Interesting Reasons Why You Should Visit Tenerife

Tenerife, the largest of Spain's Canary Islands, is one of the world's most prominent tourist attractions. Whether you're seeking for treks, bustling nightlife, marine wildlife, beaches and mountains, or even unappealing potato meals with the term 'wrinkled,' there's something for you here.

Here are 11 reasons why you should go to Tenerife!

Carnival in Tenerife

Every February, Tenerife's main city, Santa Cruz, hosts the world's second most popular carnival celebration (after Rio de Janeiro). This is one of the reasons why the cities are twinned.

The Marine Life

With 21 marine mammal species swimming off the shore, including bottlenose dolphins, sperm whales, and orcas, you'll be spoiled for choice when it comes to wildlife excursions.

The Food

You'll dine like royalty with a wonderful selection of traditional Spanish and Catalan dishes with a hint of African, French, and Arabic influences. Papas arrugadas (wrinkled potatoes), a boiling potato dish with a spicy green pepper sauce, is a favorite local delicacy.

All-Year Sunshine

With winter highs in the 20s and a maximum monthly average of 6 wet days, you'll be sure to get some sun no matter what time of year you come.

Teide Mountain

With 3 million yearly tourists, this 3,718-meter-tall volcano is Spain's highest peak and one of Europe's most frequented national parks.

Tenerife's Nightlife

Tenerife, although not as hectic as its Spanish island neighbors, is nonetheless a terrific location to let go. Veronica's Strip in Playa de las Americas is an excellent spot to start and end your journey.

Los Gigantes (The Giants)

One of the most beautiful spots in Tenerife features postcard-worthy vistas with a mountain range background that will do more than simply increase your Instagram likes. The cliffs actually shield the town from the winds, giving it the greatest temperature of any resort.

Diving

Tenerife is Europe's Hawaii, with year-round snorkeling and scuba diving options. You'll encounter trumpet fish, turtles, barracudas, parrot fish, and stingrays among other spectacular aquatic creatures.

The Masca Valley

The Masca Valley is one of the most beautiful regions of the island and an excellent spot for trekking. The Masca Walk is a 4.5-kilometer drop down the Masca Gorge and one of the world's most magnificent sky-to-sea climbs.

The Beaches

Yes, and you should view the Eiffel Tower when in Paris. The golden/volcanic beaches and warm crystal blue seas are the most apparent reasons to visit Tenerife. Dig in.

Observing the Stars

Tenerife's closeness to the equator and low light pollution levels make it ideal for magnificent starscapes at any time of year. The Starlight Foundation has named Teide National Park one of the best places in the globe for stargazing.

Top 10 Things to Know Before Visiting Tenerife:

- Tenerife is the largest of the Canary Islands, located off the coast of Africa. It has a mild climate year-round, with average temperatures ranging from 18 to 24°C (65 to 75°F). The island is known for its beautiful beaches, volcanic landscapes, and lush forests.
- There are two airports in Tenerife: Tenerife North Airport (TFS) and Tenerife South Airport (TFS). The majority of flights land in the south airport, but it is important to check which airport is closer to your accommodation when booking your flights.
- Tenerife is a popular tourist destination, so it can get crowded, especially during the summer months. If you are looking for a more relaxed vacation, you may want to consider visiting during the shoulder seasons (spring or autumn).
- The official currency in Tenerife is the euro. It is a good idea to exchange your currency for euros before you travel, as you may not be able to find many places that accept other currencies.
- The language spoken in Tenerife is Spanish. However, many people also speak English, so you should not have any problems communicating if you do not speak Spanish.

- The cost of living in Tenerife is relatively high, especially compared to other parts of Spain. This is because the island is a popular tourist destination and there is a high demand for goods and services.
- There are a variety of different places to stay in Tenerife, from budget-friendly hostels to luxury hotels. It is important to book your accommodation in advance, especially if you are traveling during the peak season.
- There are many different things to do in Tenerife, from relaxing on the beach to hiking in the mountains. If you are not sure what to do, you can ask your hotel or a local tourist information office for recommendations.
- Be aware of the local customs and laws in Tenerife. For example, it is illegal to smoke in public places and it is important to be respectful of the religious beliefs of others.

The Dos and Don'ts in Tenerife

When visiting Tenerife, it's important to respect the local customs and cultural norms. By being mindful of the dos and don'ts, you can ensure a more enjoyable and harmonious experience during your time on the island. Here are some key points to keep in mind:

Dos:

Do greet with a friendly "Hola" or "Buenos días": It's customary to greet people with a warm hello or good morning when interacting with locals, hotel staff, or shopkeepers. This simple gesture shows respect and friendliness.

Do dress appropriately: Tenerife has a relaxed atmosphere, but it's advisable to dress modestly when visiting religious sites or participating in cultural events. Cover your shoulders and knees, particularly when entering churches or during religious festivals.

Do try the local cuisine: Tenerife boasts a rich culinary heritage, so indulge in the traditional Canarian dishes and flavors. Sample fresh seafood, mojo sauces, wrinkled potatoes, and local wines. Embrace the opportunity to savor the island's gastronomic delights.

Do participate in local festivals and traditions: Tenerife is renowned for its vibrant festivals and cultural celebrations. Join in the festivities, such as the Carnival of Santa Cruz de Tenerife, and experience the island's vibrant spirit. Respect local customs and follow guidelines during these events.

Do explore beyond the tourist areas: While Tenerife has popular tourist destinations, venture off the beaten path to discover the island's hidden gems. Explore charming villages, hike through nature reserves, and engage with local communities to gain a deeper understanding of Tenerife's culture.

Don'ts:

Don't ignore beach etiquette: Tenerife's beaches are popular tourist spots, so be considerate of others. Avoid excessive noise, keep the beaches clean, and respect designated swimming areas. Nudity is not permitted on most public beaches.

Don't drink excessively in public: While enjoying Tenerife's vibrant nightlife, be mindful of alcohol consumption. Public intoxication is generally frowned upon, and excessive drinking can lead to undesirable situations. Drink responsibly and respect local laws and regulations.

Don't forget to tip appropriately: Tipping in Tenerife is customary but not obligatory. It's common to leave a 5-10% tip at restaurants, especially for good service. In bars and taxis, rounding up the bill or leaving small change is appreciated.

Don't disregard environmental conservation: Tenerife's natural beauty is a treasure to be cherished. Respect the environment by not littering, especially in nature reserves and hiking trails. Follow signage and guidelines to protect the fragile ecosystems and wildlife.

Don't underestimate the siesta tradition: Tenerife, like many Spanish regions, observes a midday siesta. During this time, some shops and businesses may close for a few hours. Plan your activities accordingly, and be aware that the pace of life might slow down during this period.

By following these dos and don'ts, you can show respect for Tenerife's culture and enhance your overall experience on the island. Embrace the local customs, engage with the community, and leave a positive impression as you immerse yourself in Tenerife's vibrant traditions and natural beauty.

CHAPTER 2: Essential Travel Information

10 Simple Steps to Planning your Next Trip

Decide when you want to go: Tenerife has a mild climate year-round, but the best time to visit is during the spring (April-May) or fall (September-October) when the weather is warm and sunny but not too hot.

Choose your activities: There are so many things to do in Tenerife, so it's important to decide what you want to focus on. Do you want to relax on the beach, explore the island's natural beauty, or go hiking and biking

Book your flights and accommodation: Once you know when you're going and what you want to do, it's time to start booking your flights and accommodation. There are a variety of airlines that fly to Tenerife, so you should be able to find a good deal. There are also many different hotels, apartments, and villas to choose from, so you can find something that fits your budget and style.

Get a travel visa if necessary: If you're not a citizen of the European Union, you may need to get a travel visa to visit Tenerife. You can apply for a visa at your local Spanish embassy or consulate.

Pack your bags: Don't forget to pack sunscreen, a hat, sunglasses, and comfortable shoes. You may also want to pack a swimsuit, a cover-up, and a light jacket if you're visiting during the shoulder seasons.

Do some research on the island: Read guidebooks, blogs, and travel articles to learn more about Tenerife's history, culture, and attractions. This will help you plan your trip and make the most of your time on the island.

Get travel insurance: Travel insurance can help protect you in case of unexpected events, such as flight cancellations, lost luggage, or medical emergencies.

Learn some Spanish phrase: Even if you don't speak fluent Spanish, learning a few basic phrases will help you get around and communicate with the locals.

Be flexible: Things don't always go according to plan when you're traveling, so it's important to be flexible. If your flight is delayed or your hotel reservation is cancelled, don't panic. Just roll with the punches and make the most of your trip.

Enjoy yourself! Tenerife is a beautiful island with so much to offer. So relax, have fun, and make the most of your trip.

Tips for avoiding the crowds in Tenerife:

- Avoid peak season (June-August): This is the busiest time of year on the island, so if you want to avoid the crowds, it's best to avoid visiting during these months.
- Choose a less popular resort: If you're looking for a more peaceful vacation, consider choosing a resort that is less popular than Playa de las Américas or Los Cristianos.
- Stay in a smaller town: There are many smaller towns on Tenerife that are less crowded than the main tourist resorts.
- Visit during the week: The island is generally less crowded during the week than on weekends.
- Do some research: There are many websites and travel blogs that can help you plan your trip and avoid the crowds

Expenses and Budgeting for Tenerife

You should budget roughly €128 ($140) each day for your holiday in Tenerife, since this is the average daily price based on previous travelers' spending. Previous visitors spent an average of €39 ($42) on meals for one day and €60 ($66) on local transportation. In addition, the average hotel fee for a couple in Tenerife is €106 ($116). So, a one-week vacation to Tenerife for two individuals costs on average €1,795 ($1,963). All of these typical travel rates were gathered from previous travelers to assist you in planning your own trip budget.

A one-week holiday in Tenerife typically costs roughly €898 for one person. So, a one-week vacation to Tenerife for two individuals costs roughly €1,795 per person. In Tenerife, a two-week holiday for two individuals costs €3,590. When traveling as a family of three or four individuals, the price per person generally decreases since children's tickets are less expensive and hotel rooms may be shared. Your daily budget will decrease if you travel slowly over a longer period of time. Two persons vacationing in Tenerife for a month may have a smaller daily budget per person than one person traveling alone for a week.

Tenerife Accommodation Budget Average Daily Costs.

The average cost of lodging in Tenerife for one person is €53. The average price paid for a hotel room in Tenerife for two persons sharing a normal double-occupancy hotel room is €106. This figure is based on real traveler expenditure.

Tenerife Hotel Rates Prices vary depending on location, date, season, and degree of luxury. See the alternatives listed below.

Tenerife Transportation Budget Average Daily Costs.

A cab journey in Tenerife is much more expensive than public transit. Previous visitors to Tenerife paid an average of €60 per person, per day on local transportation.

Tenerife Food Budget Average Daily Costs.

While meal costs in Tenerife vary, the average day's food expenditure in Tenerife is €39. Based on past tourists' spending tendencies, an average lunch in Tenerife should cost roughly €15 per person while eating out. Breakfast is usually less expensive than lunch or supper. Food costs in Tenerife sit-down restaurants are often more than quick food or street food pricing.

The Cheapest Time to Visit Tenerife

The weather is pleasant in January, with average temperatures about 21°C (70°F). There is a risk of rain, but it will be brief. In January, the island is less congested since many guests have gone home following the holiday season. This is the most affordable month to visit Tenerife, with the lowest airfare and lodging expenses.

February had similar weather to January, with average temperatures of roughly 21°C (70°F). There is a risk of rain, but it will be brief. In February, the island is still less congested since many people are still enjoying their winter vacations in other parts of the globe. This is also one of the most affordable months to visit Tenerife, since airfare and hotel expenses remain low.

March: The weather begins to warm up, with average temperatures about 23°C (73°F). Rain is still possible, although it is getting less often. The island remains less congested in March, as many visitors await the start of the spring season. If you want pleasant weather and affordable pricing, now is a fantastic time to visit Tenerife.

November: The weather remains warm and sunny, with average temperatures about 24°C (75°F). There is a minor possibility of rain, although it is quite unlikely. In November, the island begins to become less congested as visitors begin to return home for the winter. If you want pleasant weather and less tourists, now is the time to visit Tenerife.

The weather is pleasant in December, with average temperatures about 21°C (70°F). There is a risk of rain, but it will be brief. The island is less congested in December since many visitors are away for the holidays in other areas of Europe. If you want a more calm holiday, now is an excellent time to visit Tenerife.

It's crucial to remember that even during the lowest seasons, the cost of flights and accommodations might fluctuate based on the dates of your trip. Booking your tickets and accommodations ahead of time is usually a smart idea, particularly if you're going during high season.

Tenerife Entertainment Budget Average Daily Costs.

According to previous tourists' expenditures, entertainment and activities in Tenerife cost an average of €27 per person, per day. This includes museum and site admission fees, day tours, and other sightseeing expenses.

Tenerife Alcohol Budget Average Daily Costs

In Tenerife, the typical individual spends €6.43 per day on alcoholic drinks. Despite your bigger budget, the more you spend on booze, the more fun you may have.

Tenerife has long been renowned as a favorite holiday destination for Europeans. Amazing beaches and a thriving nightlife draw people from all over the world, including England, Germany, and Spain, especially over the Easter break. It's not simply a party destination for spring breakers; it also has mountains, volcanoes, and woods to explore.

How to Get to Tenerife

There are two main ways to get to Tenerife: by plane or by ferry.

By Plane

There are several airlines that fly to Tenerife from all over the world, including:

Iberia

Air Europa

British Airways

EasyJet

Ryanair

The two main airports in Tenerife are:

Tenerife North Airport (TFN)

Tenerife South Airport (TFS)

Tenerife North Airport is located in the northern part of the island, near the city of Santa Cruz de Tenerife. Tenerife South Airport is located in the southern part of the island, near the resort towns of Playa de las Américas and Los Cristianos.

By Ferry

There are several ferry companies that operate ferries to Tenerife from mainland Spain and the other Canary Islands, including

Trasmediterránea

Naviera Armas

Fred Olsen Express

The ferries from mainland Spain depart from the ports of Cádiz and Huelva. The ferries from the other Canary Islands depart from the ports of Las Palmas de Gran Canaria, Lanzarote, and Fuerteventura.

The ferry journey from mainland Spain to Tenerife takes between 9 and 11 hours. The ferry journey from the other Canary Islands to Tenerife takes between 2 and 4 hours.

Once you arrive in Tenerife, you can get around the island by car, bus, taxi, or rental bike.

Pros and cons of getting to Tenerife by plane or by ferry

Plane

Pros:

Faster

More frequent departures

More direct flights

Cons:

More expensive

Can be more crowded

Not as scenic

Ferry: Pros

Cheaper

More scenic

Can be a more relaxing journey

Cons:

Takes longer

Less frequent departures

Not as many direct flights

Ultimately, the best way to get to Tenerife depends on your individual needs and preferences. If you're looking for the fastest and most convenient option, then flying is the way to go. If you're on a budget or want a more scenic journey, then taking the ferry is a good option.

Here are some additional tips for getting to Tenerife:

- ➤ Book your flights or ferry tickets in advance, especially if you're traveling during peak season.
- ➤ Allow plenty of time to get to the airport or port, especially if you're traveling with luggage.
- ➤ Check the weather forecast before you go and pack accordingly.

- If you're taking the ferry, make sure to bring your passport and any other necessary documentation.
- Once you arrive in Tenerife, you can exchange your currency at the airport or at one of the many exchange bureaus on the island.
- If you're renting a car, make sure to have a valid driver's license and insurance.

If you're not sure where to go or what to do, ask a local for help. The people in Tenerife are very friendly and helpful.

How to Get Around in Tenerife

Bus: The bus system in Tenerife is extensive and affordable. You can buy tickets at any bus stop or at the TITSA office. A single ticket costs €1.45, and a day pass costs €10.

Taxi: Taxis are a convenient way to get around, but they can be expensive. The base fare is €2.40, and the fare increases by €0.30 for every 100 meters.

Rental car: If you want to have more freedom to explore the island, you can rent a car. There are many car rental companies located in Tenerife, and prices start from around €20 per day.

Tram: The tram system in Tenerife is a modern and efficient way to get around the capital city, Santa Cruz de Tenerife. A single ticket costs €1.45, and a day pass costs €5.

Funicular: The funicular is a cable car that takes you up to the top of Mount Teide, the highest peak in Spain. A single ticket costs €9, and a return ticket costs €18.

Teleférico: The teleférico is a cable car that takes you up to the top of Mount Teide National Park. A single ticket costs €27, and a return ticket costs €42.

Tips for Getting around in Tenerife:

- If you're planning on using public transportation, buy a Bonocard. This is a rechargeable card that gives you discounted fares on buses, trams, and the funicular.
- If you're staying in a resort area, there may be a shuttle bus that can take you to nearby attractions.
- If you're going to be doing a lot of hiking or exploring the outdoors, consider renting a car or taking a taxi.
- If you're on a budget, you can also walk or bike around the city.
- Be aware of the local traffic laws and customs.

- Always use a designated taxi stand or app to hail a taxi.
- Be prepared for the heat and sun, especially if you're planning on doing outdoor activities.
- Drink plenty of water and wear sunscreen.
- Bring a hat and sunglasses.
- If you're hiking, wear sturdy shoes and bring plenty of water and snacks.
- Let someone know where you're going and when you expect to be back.

Some pros and cons of each Means of Going Around

Bus: Pros: Inexpensive, extensive network, can get you to most places on the island.

Cons: Can be crowded, can take longer than other options, not as convenient as taxis or rental cars.

Taxi: Pros: Convenient, can get you anywhere on the island quickly.

Cons: Expensive, can be difficult to hail taxis in some areas, not as environmentally friendly as public transportation.

Rental car: Pros: Freedom to explore the island at your own pace, can go to places that public transportation doesn't reach.

Cons: Can be expensive, can be difficult to drive in unfamiliar areas, parking can be difficult in some areas.

Tram: Pros: Efficient way to get around the capital city, Santa Cruz de Tenerife.

Cons: Network is not as extensive as the bus network, doesn't reach all parts of the island.

Funicular: Pros: Quick and easy way to get to the top of Mount Teide.

Cons: Can be crowded, tickets can be expensive, not wheelchair accessible.

Teleférico: Pros: Quick and easy way to get to the top of Mount Teide National Park.

Cons: Tickets can be expensive, not wheelchair accessible.

Ultimately, the best way to get around in Tenerife depends on your individual needs and preferences. If you're on a budget, public transportation is a good option. If you want to have more freedom and flexibility, a rental car is a better choice. If you're visiting the capital city, the tram is a good option for getting around quickly and easily. And if you're looking for a unique and scenic experience, the funicular or teleférico are great ways to get to the top of Mount Teide.

The Best Time to Visit Tenerife

Spring (April-May): The weather is warm and sunny, but not too hot. The average temperature is around 23°C (73°F). There are fewer tourists than in the summer, so it's a good time to visit if you want to avoid the crowds.

Autumn (September-October): The weather is still warm and sunny, with average temperatures of around 24°C (75°F). The crowds have started to thin out, so it's a good time to visit if you want to enjoy the island's beaches and attractions without the hustle and bustle of summer.

Winter (December-February): The weather is mild, with average temperatures of around 21°C (70°F). There is a chance of rain, but it's usually short-lived. The island is less crowded in the winter, so it's a good time to visit if you're looking for a more peaceful vacation.

If you're planning on visiting Tenerife for specific activities, here are some other things to consider:

Hiking and mountaineering: The best time to go hiking and mountaineering is during the spring and autumn, when the weather is mild and there are fewer crowds.

Water sports: The best time to go swimming, surfing, and other water sports is during the summer, when the weather is warm and sunny.

Snow sports: If you're interested in skiing or snowboarding, the best time to visit is during the winter, when the slopes are open.

If you're looking for warm weather and plenty of sunshine, any time of year is a good time to visit. But if you want to avoid the crowds and enjoy the island's natural beauty, spring, autumn, and winter are the best times to go.

Least crowded times to visit Tenerife:

January: The weather is mild, with average temperatures of around 21°C (70°F). There is a chance of rain, but it's usually short-lived. The island is less crowded in January, as many tourists have returned home after the holiday season.

February: The weather is similar to January, with average temperatures of around 21°C (70°F). There is a chance of rain, but it's usually short-lived. The island is still less crowded in February, as many tourists are still enjoying the winter holidays in other parts of the world.

March: The weather starts to warm up in March, with average temperatures of around 23°C (73°F). There is still a chance of rain, but it's becoming less frequent. The island is still less crowded in March, as many tourists are waiting for the start of the spring season.

April: The weather is warm and sunny in April, with average temperatures of around 24°C (75°F). There is still a chance of rain, but it's becoming very rare. The island is starting to get busier in April, as tourists start to arrive for the spring season.

May: The weather is warm and sunny in May, with average temperatures of around 25°C (77°F). There is very little chance of rain. The island is getting busier in May, as tourists start to arrive for the summer season.

If you're looking to avoid the crowds, these are the best times to visit Tenerife. However, it's important to note that even during these times, the island can still be busy, especially in popular tourist destinations such as Playa de las Américas and Los Cristianos.

Money-saving Tips for your Vacation to Tenerife:

- Consider traveling into a different airport: You may be able to discover cheaper tickets if you are prepared to fly into a different airport. Tenerife North Airport (TFN), for example, is situated in the northern section of the island and is often less expensive to fly into than Tenerife South Airport (TFS).
- Make a reservation for your lodging in advance: You may be able to obtain a better rate if you book your accommodations ahead of time. Discounts are often available on websites like as Booking.com and Hotels.com.
- Avoid high season: If you can go during the shoulder seasons (April-May and September-October), you will most certainly find lower pricing on flights and lodging.
- Stay at a hostel: If money is an issue, try staying in a hostel. Hostels provide communal dorms and toilets and are an excellent place to meet other visitors.
- Cook your own meals: If you're living in an apartment or villa, preparing your own meals may help you save money. On the island, there are several food shops where you can get fresh fruit and other items.
- Take public transportation: If you're staying in a resort area, you may be able to stroll or bike about. However, if

you want to explore the island, you need get a bus ticket. Buses are an inexpensive and convenient method to navigate about Tenerife.

- ➢ Conduct some research: There are several websites and travel blogs that may assist you in planning your vacation and saving money. You can get the greatest rates on flights, lodging, and activities by doing some research

Visa Requirements to Tenerife

Tenerife, being part of Spain and the Canary Islands, has different visa requirements based on your country, as well as the purpose and length of your stay. To guarantee a smooth entrance into Tenerife, it is important to understand the visa restrictions before organizing your vacation. The following is a comprehensive overview to the visa requirements for visiting Tenerife:

Schengen Visa: a. General Information: Tenerife is part of the Schengen Area, a group of 26 European nations that share a visa policy. If you are not a citizen of a country exempt from the Schengen visa requirement, you will need to get a Schengen visa in order to visit Tenerife.

Exemptions from the Schengen Visa: Certain nations' citizens, notably European Union (EU) member states, the United States, Canada, Australia, New Zealand, Japan, and many more, do not need a visa for visits of up to 90 days during a 180-day period. However, since exemptions might vary, it is always a good idea to verify the most recent visa requirements for your individual nationality.

Visitors from countries that have a visa-free agreement with the Schengen Area may visit Tenerife without a visa and remain for up to 90 days during a 180-day period. This covers nationals of the visa-free nations listed above.

a. Valid Passport: For visa-free entry, a valid passport is needed. It must be valid for at least three months after your departure from Tenerife. Check that your passport has enough blank pages for immigration stamps.

Long-remain Visas: a. More than 90 days: If you want to remain in Tenerife for more than 90 days, depending on your purpose of travel, you may need to apply for a long-stay visa or residency permit. Long-term visas are often necessary for job, study, or family reunion. It's important to get in touch with the Spanish consulate or embassy in your home country well in advance to learn about the precise criteria and processes for acquiring a long-stay visa.

a. Spanish Consulate/Embassy: To get a Schengen visa or long-stay visa, you must apply at the Spanish consulate or embassy in your home country. A completed application form, passport-size pictures, a valid passport, evidence of travel insurance, proof of lodging, financial papers, and a travel itinerary may be required as part of the application process.

a. Appointment: To submit your visa application, you must usually make an appointment with the consulate or embassy. Appointment availability and processing dates might vary, so prepare ahead of time for your visa application.

Visa Extension: a. If you are already in Tenerife and want to remain longer than the 90-day limit, you may be able to apply for a visa extension or a residence permit. To learn more about the procedure and conditions for visa extensions, contact the Spanish immigration authorities or a local immigration office.

It's important to note that visa requirements and regulations can change, so for the most up-to-date and accurate information on visa requirements for Tenerife, visit the official website of the Spanish Ministry of Foreign Affairs or contact the Spanish consulate or embassy in your home country.

Knowing the Tenerife visa requirements is critical for a trouble-free vacation. Whether you are qualified for visa-free entrance, a Schengen visa, or a long-stay visa, familiarizing yourself with the appropriate processes and papers will guarantee a smooth voyage to experience Tenerife's breathtaking scenery, lively culture, and kind hospitality.

CHAPTER 3: Where to Stay in Tenerife.

Accommodation Options in Tenerife

Tenerife has a variety of lodging alternatives to accommodate a variety of budgets, interests, and travel patterns. Whether you're looking for opulent resorts, charming flats, or budget-friendly guesthouses, the island has a wide range of options. Here is a thorough overview of Tenerife's lodging options:

Hotels & Resorts:

a. Luxury Resorts: Tenerife is well-known for its opulent resorts, which provide top-notch amenities such as spa facilities, several dining choices, swimming pools, and direct beach access. Many of these resorts are in well-known tourist destinations including Costa Adeje, Playa de las Américas, and Los Cristianos.

b. Mid-Range Hotels: Tenerife also has a large variety of mid-range hotels that provide pleasant lodging, accessible locations, and needed facilities. These hotels offer to a wide range of prices and are spread over the island, enabling visitors to select acceptable alternatives depending on their favourite locations.

c. Boutique and Design Hotels: Tenerife has boutique and design hotels that provide customized service, distinctive décor, and a beautiful ambiance for people looking for unique and attractive lodgings. These hotels often highlight local culture and provide a more intimate and genuine experience.

Apartments & Villas:

a. Self-Catering Apartments: Tenerife has a wide range of self-catering apartments, from studios to multi-bedroom units. These apartments include kitchenettes or complete kitchens, so visitors may make their meals and enjoy the flexibility of a home-away-from-home feel.

b. Villas and Vacation Rentals: If you want more room and solitude, Tenerife has a plethora of villas and vacation rentals to choose from. These homes often have private pools, gardens, and breathtaking views. They are great for families, parties of friends, or those seeking a private getaway.

Traditional B&Bs: Tenerife boasts wonderful bed and breakfast lodgings, notably in the rural and agricultural districts. These bed and breakfasts provide nice accommodations, fresh meals, and a warm and inviting ambiance. They are a fantastic way to experience local hospitality and immerse yourself in the island's culture.

Hostels & Guesthouses:

a. Budget-Friendly Options: Budget-conscious travelers will find reasonable lodging at Tenerife's hostels and guesthouses. These low-cost solutions often provide dormitory-style accommodations or individual rooms with shared utilities. In major tourist regions, hostels and guesthouses are common and provide a chance to meet other tourists.

Camping: a. campsites: Tenerife has various campsites with facilities for tents and camper vans for outdoor lovers. These campsites are often well-kept and located in attractive areas, enabling guests to enjoy the island's natural beauty while also engaging in outdoor activities.

Consider variables such as location, accessibility to attractions or beaches, accessible facilities, and your budget when selecting

Tenerife lodging. It is best to book ahead of time, particularly during high seasons, to ensure your preferred option.

Tenerife also boasts a number of all-inclusive resorts that provide extensive packages that include lodgings, food, beverages, and entertainment. These resorts are especially popular for family holidays since they provide a hassle-free experience.

FTenerife has rural guesthouses, fincas (farmhouses), and eco-friendly hotels for people looking for a more genuine and immersive experience. These choices enable tourists to interact with nature, learn about local customs, and relax in the island's countryside.

Things to consider before booking Accommodation Tenerife

When planning a trip to Tenerife, it's important to carefully consider your accommodation options to ensure a comfortable and enjoyable stay on the island. Here are some key factors to consider before booking your accommodation in Tenerife:

Location:

Proximity to Attractions: Consider the location of your accommodation in relation to the attractions and activities you plan to experience in Tenerife. If you're interested in beach life, choose a hotel or apartment near the coast. For hiking and nature exploration, accommodations closer to the mountains or rural areas might be more suitable.

Accessibility: Take into account the accessibility of your accommodation in terms of transportation links, proximity to public transport, and convenience for exploring the island. Consider whether you prefer a quieter location or a more lively area with restaurants, shops, and nightlife.

Budget:

Determine your budget for accommodation and search for options that fit within your financial constraints. Tenerife offers a wide range of accommodations catering to different budgets, from luxury resorts to budget-friendly hostels and apartments.

Remember to factor in additional costs such as meals, transportation, and activities when assessing the overall affordability of your chosen accommodation.

Amenities and Facilities:

Assess the amenities and facilities offered by the accommodation. Consider whether you need specific features such as a swimming pool, fitness center, spa, on-site restaurants, or free Wi-Fi.

If you're traveling with family, check if the accommodation provides child-friendly amenities, such as playgrounds or family rooms.

For those who require accessibility features or have special needs, ensure that the accommodation can cater to your requirements.

Reviews and Ratings:

Read reviews and ratings from previous guests to get an understanding of their experiences with the accommodation. Websites like TripAdvisor, Booking.com, and Google Reviews provide valuable insights into the quality and service of accommodations.

Pay attention to recent reviews to ensure that the information is up to date and relevant. Look for consistent positive feedback on cleanliness, staff friendliness, and overall guest satisfaction.

Booking Policies and Flexibility:

Understand the booking policies of the accommodation, including cancellation policies, refundable or non-refundable rates, and any additional charges or fees.

Check the flexibility of the accommodation regarding date changes or modifications, as unexpected situations or travel plans may arise.

Safety and Security:

Consider the safety and security measures in place at the accommodation. Look for features such as secure entrances, surveillance cameras, and in-room safes.

Research the overall safety of the neighborhood or area where the accommodation is located, particularly if you plan to venture out during the evenings.

Additional Services:

Determine if you require any additional services, such as airport transfers, car rental assistance, or tour bookings. Some accommodations offer these services or can provide recommendations.

By carefully considering these factors, you can select accommodation in Tenerife that aligns with your preferences, budget, and travel plans. Taking the time to research and evaluate your options will contribute to a more enjoyable and fulfilling experience on the captivating island of Tenerife.

Luxury Hotels and Resorts in Tenerife

Hotel Botanico & The Oriental Spa Garden: This 5-star hotel is at Puerto de la Cruz, on Tenerife's north coast. It boasts a lovely garden, an infinity pool with panoramic views, and a world-class spa. Rooms begin around €300 per night.

Gran Hotel Atlantis La Caleta: This 5-star hotel is situated in Costa Adeje, on Tenerife's southern shore. It boasts a private beach, an infinity pool on the roof, and a Michelin-starred restaurant. Rooms begin around €400 per night.

Hotel Jardn Tropical: This 5-star hotel is situated in Playa de las Américas on Tenerife's south coast. There is a tropical garden, a water park, and a casino on the premises. Rooms begin from €500 per night.

Hotel Ritz-Carlton Abama: This 5-star hotel is situated in Gua de Isora, on Tenerife's south coast. It is situated on a clifftop with breathtaking views of the Atlantic Ocean. Rooms begin around €600 per night.

Hotel Royal Hideaway Corales Beach: This 5-star hotel is situated in Costa Adeje, on Tenerife's southern coast. It offers a private beach, a lagoon pool, and a spa. Rooms begin around €700 per night.

Hotel Bahia del Duque: This 5-star hotel is situated on Costa Adeje, on Tenerife's south coast. It boasts its own beach, golf course, and spa. Rooms begin around €800 per night.

Mid-Range Hotels and Resorts in Tenerife

Hotel Vincci Selección La Plantación del Sur: This 4-star hotel is at Costa Adeje, on Tenerife's south coast. There's a pool, a fitness center, and a bar with live music. Rooms begin around €150 per night.

Hotel H10 Tenerife Playa La Américas: This 4-star hotel is situated on Tenerife's south coast in Playa de las Américas. There's a pool, a fitness center, and a bar with live music. Rooms begin about €100 per night.

Tigaiga Princess Hotel: This 4-star hotel is situated in Puerto de la Cruz, on Tenerife's north coast. There's a pool, a fitness center, and a bar with live music. Rooms begin about €120 per night.

The Senses Luxury Resort & Spa: This 4-star hotel is situated in Adeje, on Tenerife's south coast. It has a pool, a workout center, and a spa. Rooms begin about €130 per night.

Sercotel Cristina: This 4-star hotel is situated in Puerto de la Cruz, on Tenerife's north coast. There's a pool, a fitness center, and a bar with live music. Rooms begin around €140 per night.

Budget friendly Hotels and Resorts in Tenerife

Hostel One Tenerife is situated in Santa Cruz de Tenerife, the island's capital. It offers a communal kitchen, a common area with a TV, and a rooftop terrace with city views. Dorm beds cost around €20 per night.

Oasis Backpackers: This hostel is situated in Playa de las Américas, on Tenerife's south coast. It offers a communal kitchen, a TV in the common area, and a rooftop patio with views of the beach. Dorm beds cost around €15 per night.

Hostel Jardn del Sol: This hostel is situated in Puerto de la Cruz, on Tenerife's north coast. It offers a communal kitchen, a common area with a TV, and a roof terrace with city views. Dorm beds cost around €10 per night.

Best Areas to Stay in Tenerife

Costa Adeje is a lively resort in the south and one of the best places to stay for families in Tenerife. It has a wide range of hotels, apartments, and villas to choose from, as well as plenty of restaurants, bars, and shops. The beaches in Costa Adeje are some of the best on the island, and there are also many opportunities for water sports, such as windsurfing, sailing, and diving.

Playa de las Americas is another popular resort in the south of Tenerife. It is known for its lively nightlife and its many bars and clubs. There are also a number of water parks in Playa de las Americas, making it a great destination for families.

Los Cristianos is a more laid-back resort than Playa de las Americas, but it still has plenty to offer visitors. It has a beautiful beach, a lively harbor, and a number of restaurants and shops. Los Cristianos is also a good base for exploring the south of Tenerife, as it is well-connected to other resorts by bus.

Puerto de la Cruz is a charming town in the north of Tenerife. It has a historic center, a beautiful botanical garden, and a number of black sand beaches. Puerto de la Cruz is a popular destination for families, couples, and older travelers.

El Medano is a small town in the south of Tenerife. It is known for its windsurfing and kitesurfing, and it is a popular destination for those who enjoy water sports. El Medano is also a good place to relax and enjoy the beach.

Los Gigantes is a town in the west of Tenerife. It is known for its towering cliffs, which offer stunning views of the Atlantic Ocean. Los Gigantes is a popular destination for couples and those who enjoy hiking and water sports.

Puerto Santiago is a small town in the west of Tenerife. It is a quieter alternative to Los Gigantes, and it is a popular destination for those who enjoy relaxing on the beach.

Callao Salvaje is a small town in the west of Tenerife. It is a quiet and secluded destination, and it is a popular destination for those who enjoy hiking and fishing.

La Caleta is a small town in the south of Tenerife. It is a quiet and relaxed destination, and it is a popular destination for those who enjoy hiking and whale watching.

La Laguna is a historic city in the north of Tenerife. It is a UNESCO World Heritage Site, and it is a popular destination for those who enjoy history and culture.

These are just a few of the best areas to stay in Tenerife. There are many other great places to choose from, so you are sure to find the perfect place to suit your needs and budget.

Some Neighborhoods to Avoid in Tenerife

Las Galletas: This town is located in the south of Tenerife and is known for its budget-friendly accommodation. However, it can also be a bit seedy and there have been reports of petty crime in the area.

El Médano: This town is also located in the south of Tenerife and is a popular destination for windsurfing and kitesurfing. However, it can be windy and chilly in the winter, and the beaches can be crowded.

Arona: This municipality is located in the south of Tenerife and is home to a number of popular resorts. However, it can be very crowded, especially in the summer months.

La Laguna: This city is located in the north of Tenerife and is a UNESCO World Heritage Site. However, it can be quite expensive to stay in La Laguna, and it is not as well-connected to other parts of the island as some other areas.

It is important to note that these are just a few areas to avoid in Tenerife. There are many other great places to stay on the island, so you are sure to find the perfect place to suit your needs and budget.

Tips for Avoiding Trouble in Tenerife:

- Be aware of your surroundings and take precautions against petty crime.
- Avoid walking alone at night, especially in secluded areas.
- Be careful about what you leave in your car, as break-ins are not uncommon.
- If you are planning on hiking, be sure to let someone know where you are going and when you expect to be back.
- Drink responsibly and be aware of your surroundings if you are out at night.

By following these tips, you can help to ensure a safe and enjoyable stay in Tenerife.

Tenerife 3-Day Itinerary:

Day 1: In the morning:

Begin the day by visiting Teide National Park. Take a cable car to the peak of Mount Teide for amazing views.

Hike the park's paths and marvel at the unusual volcanic sceneries.

Afternoon:

Travel to La Orotava, a medieval town. Explore its lovely streets and marvel at the classic Canarian architecture.

Explore the lovely balconies embellished with delicate woodwork at the famed Casa de los Balcones.

Evening:

In Puerto de la Cruz, a bustling seaside town famed for its outstanding dining choices, treat yourself to a delicious evening.

Take a walk down the promenade and enjoy the sea breeze.

Day 2: In the morning:

Take a boat tour to see dolphins and whales in their natural environment. These trips are available from a number of tour companies departing from different ports.

While taking in the scenery, trained experts will teach you about the wonderful marine creatures.

Afternoon:

Visit the charming village of Garachico. Visit its picturesque alleyways, the medieval castle, and the natural rock pools.

Don't pass up the chance to sample some delectable local ice cream at one of the artisanal ice cream establishments.

Evening:

Visit the island's capital, Santa Cruz de Tenerife. Explore the colorful city center, pay a visit to the renowned Auditorio de Tenerife, and dine at a local restaurant.

Day 3: In the morning:

Relax on one of Tenerife's lovely beaches in the morning. The golden sand at Playa de Las Teresitas is a popular option.

Take a plunge in the clean waters or just relax in the sun.

Afternoon:

Explore Masca, a lovely hamlet set in the Teno Mountains. Enjoy a picturesque stroll through Masca Gorge with spectacular views of the neighboring regions.

Evening:

In a neighborhood restaurant, have a classic Canarian meal. Prepared foods such as papas arrugadas (wrinkled potatoes) with mojo sauce and freshly grilled seafood are available.

Tenerife Itinerary for 7 Days:

Day 1: Arrival and Unwinding

After arriving in Tenerife, spend the day settling in and seeing the surrounding region.

Relax on a local beach, go for a refreshing dip, and absorb up the relaxed environment of the island.

Day 2: Exploring Nature Morning:

Start your day by visiting Teide National Park. Take the cable car to Mount Teide's peak for panoramic views of the island.

Afternoon:

Hike the park's hiking paths, such as the Roques de Garca trail, and marvel at the park's distinctive volcanic vistas.

Evening:

Spend an evening relaxing at a local restaurant, enjoying traditional Canarian cuisine and relishing the island's gastronomic wonders.

Morning of Day 3: Cultural Exploration

Visit the UNESCO World Heritage-listed village of La Laguna. Discover its picturesque streets, museums, and colonial buildings.

Afternoon:

Visit the Museum of Nature and Man or the Museum of Science and the Cosmos to learn about the island's cultural legacy.

Evening:

Experience the bustling arts scene of Santa Cruz de Tenerife by attending a cultural performance or live music event.

Day 4: Coastal Adventure

Morning:

Take a leisurely drive along the TF-5 highway, pausing at vistas to take in the gorgeous coastline scenery.

Afternoon:

Visit the charming town of Garachico and learn about its history, which includes the Castle of San Miguel and natural rock pools.

Evening:

Enjoy a quiet evening at Puerto de la Cruz, a seaside village. Take a stroll down the promenade before dining at a coastal restaurant.

Day 5: Wildlife and Adventure

Morning:

Set off from Los Cristianos or Los Gigantes for a whale and dolphin viewing expedition. Admire these amazing animals in their natural environment.

Afternoon:

Siam Park, a world-famous water park with exciting slides, meandering rivers, and soothing pool areas, is a must-see.

Evening:

Dine at one of the beachfront restaurants in Los Cristianos or Los Abrigos, relishing fresh seafood and regional cuisine.

Day 6: North Exploration Morning:

Visit the lovely Anaga Rural Park in the island's northernmost region. Hike through its lush woodlands and take in the breathtaking scenery.

Afternoon:

Explore La Orotava, a picturesque village famed for its well-preserved medieval center and magnificent gardens.

Evening:

Visit a vineyard or bodega in the Tacoronte area to sample local wines and traditional Canarian food.

Day 7: Beaches and Farewell Breakfast:

Spend the morning lounging at Playa de Las Teresitas, a lovely golden sand beach near Santa Cruz de Tenerife.

Afternoon:

Snorkeling or scuba diving at one of Tenerife's prominent diving areas is a great way to explore the underwater world.

Evening:

Enjoy a goodbye supper at one of Tenerife's best dining venues while thinking on the fantastic experiences and memories you had while on the island.

CHAPTER 4: Food, Dinning and Night Life

Canarian Traditional Dishes

As part of the Canary Islands, Tenerife has a diverse culinary tradition inspired by Spanish, Latin American, and indigenous Guanche cuisines. Exploring traditional Canarian cuisine is an enjoyable excursion into the island's distinct gastronomy. Here are some traditional Canarian delicacies not to be missed:

Papas Arrugadas: This traditional Canarian meal comprises of tiny, salted potatoes cooked in their peel till soft. The potatoes are often served with one of two varieties of spicy sauces known as mojo: red mojo (made with paprika) and green mojo (made with coriander or parsley). The dish gets its name from the wrinkled look of the potatoes ("arrugadas" means wrinkled).

Gofio is a traditional Canarian flour produced from roasted grains, most often wheat or maize. For ages, it has been a staple of the Canarian diet. Gofio may be eaten as a basic paste combined with water or milk, or it can be used as an ingredient in a variety of recipes or desserts. It is very healthy and is often served as a side or topping to other cuisines.

Puchero Canario is a hearty stew that symbolizes the island's heritage and agricultural bounty. It includes a range of meats, including beef, poultry, and pig, as well as vegetables like as carrots, potatoes, cabbage, and chickpeas. Spices and herbs enhance the tastes, resulting in a soothing and flavorful dinner.

Conejo en Salmorejo: This Canarian rabbit dish is marinated in a salmorejo sauce composed with garlic, vinegar, olive oil, paprika, and other fragrant seasonings. The rabbit is marinated for many hours before cooking, resulting in soft and delicious flesh. It is often served with arrugadas and mojo sauce.

Sancocho Canario: Sancocho is a traditional Canarian meal served on special occasions. It's made with salted fish, generally cod, and potatoes, sweet potatoes, and veggies. The meal is well-known for its simplicity and unique tastes. Each component is cooked separately before being blended to provide a filling and delectable dinner.

Bienmesabe: Bienmesabe is a Canarian dessert that literally means "tastes good to me." It's a delicious almond cream prepared with ground almonds, sugar, egg yolks, lemon zest, and cinnamon. This creamy, fragrant delicacy is often served cold and topped with toasted almonds.

Mojo Sauce: Mojo sauces are a staple of Canarian cuisine and are used with a variety of foods. Red mojo (mojo rojo) and green mojo (mojo verde) are the two most frequent varieties. The red mojo is usually hot, and it is produced using red peppers, garlic, paprika, vinegar, and olive oil. Green peppers, garlic, coriander or parsley, cumin, vinegar, and olive oil are used in the green mojo, which is milder. Many Canarian foods benefit from the addition of these tasty sauces.

When visiting Tenerife, be sure to try these classic Canarian meals to fully appreciate the island's gastronomic offerings. Many local restaurants and diners provide real Canarian food, enabling you to experience the distinct tastes and fragrances handed down through generations.

Well-known Restaurants and Cafés

As a bustling and diversified location, Tenerife has a vast range of food alternatives to suit every taste and budget. From traditional Canarian fare to worldwide cuisines, the island's restaurants and cafés will please even the most discriminating palates. Here are some popular restaurants to visit when on vacation in Tenerife:

Restaurante El Rincón de Juan Carlos (Los Gigantes): Known for its unique and artistic approach to Canarian food, this Michelin-starred restaurant in Los Gigantes is a must-visit. The cuisine mixes traditional tastes with contemporary methods, resulting in outstanding dishes that represent the island's culinary history, with a concentration on locally produced products.

Restaurante Kazan (Santa Cruz de Tenerife): A must-visit for sushi and seafood enthusiasts, Restaurante Kazan offers a blend of Japanese and Canarian cuisine. The cuisine combines fresh local ingredients with traditional Japanese methods to create a harmonious and one-of-a-kind eating experience.

La Casona del Vino (El Sauzal): La Casona del Vino is a lovely restaurant that highlights Tenerife's cuisine. It is located in the scenic village of El Sauzal. The restaurant, known for its superb wine selection, has a quiet environment and a cuisine that features classic Canarian foods served with a contemporary touch.

La Hierbita (La Laguna): A hidden treasure in the ancient city of La Laguna, La Hierbita is famed for its tapas and authentic Canarian food. In a casual and inviting atmosphere, the restaurant highlights local tastes and ingredients. Don't pass up the chance to taste their legendary papas arrugadas with mojo sauce.

El Taller Seve Diaz (Puerto de la Cruz): El Taller Seve Diaz, led by famous chef Seve Diaz, is a gourmet hotspot in Puerto de la Cruz. Traditional Canarian recipes are combined with modern technology to create unique and aesthetically attractive meals that tickle the taste sensations.

El Patio del Loro (Garachico): El Patio del Loro, located in the lovely village of Garachico, provides a great eating experience in a gorgeous courtyard setting. The cuisine emphasizes fresh fish and local products that are masterfully cooked to highlight the tastes of Tenerife.

Café de Paris (Playa de las Américas): Café de Paris, located in the busy Playa de las Américas, is a favorite destination for both residents and visitors. This French-inspired café serves a variety of pastries, sweets, and sandwiches, as well as fragrant coffees and refreshing drinks. It's a great spot for a leisurely breakfast or an afternoon snack.

La Pepa Food Market (Santa Cruz de Tenerife): Visit La Pepa Food Market in Santa Cruz for a one-of-a-kind gastronomic experience. This lively food market has a wide range of vendors where you may enjoy local delicacies, foreign cuisine, and fresh products. There's something for everyone's taste, from tapas to sushi.

These are just a handful of Tenerife's numerous outstanding restaurants and cafés. Whether you're looking for gourmet dining, traditional Canarian cuisine, cosmopolitan cuisines, or informal cafes, the island has a multitude of possibilities to suit your gastronomic desires. Remember to look into local suggestions, examine travel books, and ask locals for ideas to find hidden culinary jewels during your time in Tenerife.

Local Markets and Street Food

Exploring Tenerife's street food scene and local markets is an excellent opportunity to get acquainted with the island's cuisine and culture. These culinary places give a colorful and genuine sense of Tenerife, from tempting appetizers to fresh products. Here are some highlights of the street food scene and local markets to try while you're there:

Mercado de Nuestra Seora de Africa (Santa Cruz de Tenerife): This lively market in the center of Santa Cruz is a foodie's heaven. It is known as La Recova and provides a large variety of fresh products, including locally produced fruits, vegetables, herbs, and spices. There are also vendors offering cheese, sausage, fish, and other traditional items. Take advantage of the chance to sample local specialties such as queso fresco (fresh cheese) and Canarian bananas.

Mercado de la Laguna (San Cristóbal de La Laguna): This lively market in La Laguna highlights the variety of Tenerife's native goods. Explore the kiosks loaded with vibrant fruits and veggies, handmade bread, honey, and more. There are also street food booths where you may try classic Canarian cuisine like empanadas (stuffed pastries), churros, and bocadillos (sandwiches).

Mercadillo del Agricultor de Tacoronte (Tacoronte): This farmers' market in Tacoronte, held every Saturday and Sunday, provides a real farm-to-table experience. Visit the vendors selling fresh fruits and veggies, herbs, handmade jams, and baked items.

Try the almogrote (a cheese spread), gofio-based delicacies, and traditional pastries.

Street Food in Playa de las Américas: Street food is popular in the busy tourist destination of Playa de las Américas. Explore the beachside promenades for food vendors and kiosks selling a wide range of snacks and delicacies. The legendary bocadillos de calamares (fried squid sandwiches), churros with hot chocolate, and cool tropical fruit drinks are also must-tries.

Fiesta del Vino of La Orotava: If you chance to be in La Orotava during the annual Fiesta del Vino, you'll have the opportunity to indulge in street cuisine pleasures. This wine festival highlights local wine production and includes kiosks offering traditional Canarian foods and refreshments. Tapas, grilled meats, and delectable desserts are coupled with the best wines on the island.

Food Truck Festivals and gourmet Events: Food truck festivals and gourmet events are held all over the island. These gatherings bring together a wide range of local merchants selling anything from traditional Canarian cuisine to foreign delicacies. During your vacation, look for local event listings or ask locals for ideas.

It's crucial to exercise excellent hygiene and select vendors with clean and well-maintained booths while eating street food and visiting local markets. Try new tastes and interact with merchants to learn more about their goods and culinary traditions.

Exploring Tenerife's street food scene and local markets connects you with the island's dynamic food culture and enables you to explore the different flavors that make the Canary Islands a gastronomic destination worth visiting.

Dietary Restrictions and Special Requirements

Tenerife understands the significance of accommodating varied dietary restrictions and unique needs. Whether you have dietary limitations due to allergies, religious beliefs, or personal preferences, the island has a wide variety of culinary alternatives to meet your requirements. Here are some things to think about and tips for a memorable dining experience in Tenerife:

Vegan and vegetarian

Vegetarian-Friendly Restaurants: Tenerife is home to an increasing number of vegetarian-friendly restaurants serving plant-based cuisine. Look for restaurants that clearly indicate their vegetarian offerings or that specialize in vegetarian and vegan food.

Vegan and vegetarian markets: Visit local markets like Mercado de Nuestra Seora de Africa in Santa Cruz to discover fresh fruits and vegetables as well as plant-based items to cook your meals or snacks.

Many foreign restaurants in Tenerife, notably those providing Mediterranean, Indian, and Asian food, provide vegetarian and vegan alternatives on their menus.

Gluten-Free:

Gluten-Free Awareness: Gluten-free diets are becoming more popular in Tenerife, and more eateries are adjusting to meet this dietary necessity. Look for eateries that provide gluten-free menus or alternatives.

Celiac-Friendly Restaurants: Some restaurants have dedicated gluten-free kitchens or particular standards in place to reduce cross-contamination. In ahead, do research and contact establishments to enquire about their gluten-free options and cooking processes.

Food Allergies and Intolerances:

Communication: When eating out, advise the restaurant personnel of any allergies or intolerances you may have. Discuss your demands with them, and they will be able to advise you on appropriate solutions or make alterations to meet your needs.

Ingredient Knowledge: Keep an eye out for common allergies in foods and components. Inquire about particular ingredients used in recipes to ensure they are free of allergies that might cause a response.

Self-Catering Options: If you have severe allergies or dietary intolerances, consider staying in a place that has a kitchen. This enables you to cook meals using components you know and trust while avoiding possible hazards.

Halal and Kosher certification:

Tenerife offers a limited selection of Halal and Kosher restaurants. Some foreign restaurants, however, may provide Halal or Kosher-certified cuisine. It is recommended that you call the businesses ahead of time to learn about their special services.

Self-Catering: For more stringent adherence to Halal or Kosher dietary needs, consider self-catering lodgings, where you have complete control over cooking and item selection.

Communicating Dietary Requirements:

While many restaurants and hotels in tourist locations have English-speaking personnel, it's useful to learn a few basic words in Spanish to successfully convey your dietary preferences.

Allergen Cards: Carry allergen cards printed in Spanish if you have severe allergies or experience language challenges. These cards clearly describe your dietary restrictions or allergies, assisting you in communicating your requirements to restaurant personnel.

To guarantee a safe and happy eating experience in Tenerife, remember to plan ahead, study acceptable meal alternatives, and discuss your dietary preferences with restaurant employees. Being proactive in your approach can help you uncover culinary alternatives that cater to your individual needs, enabling you to enjoy the island's various tastes.

Nightclubs and Bars

Tenerife is recognized for its bustling and active nightlife, with a wide variety of pubs and nightclubs to satisfy a wide range of interests and preferences. The island has enough to offer, whether you want a calm evening drink or a night full with dance and excitement. Here's a list of Tenerife's pubs and nightclubs:

The American Beach:

Veronicas Strip: Veronicas Strip, located in Playa de las Américas, is a popular nightlife destination noted for its various bars and clubs. It aims to a younger audience by delivering a variety of music genres such as pop, dance, and electronic music. After midnight, the strip comes alive with DJs and live entertainment at pubs and clubs.

Adeje Costa:

Puerto Colón: Puerto Colón, located in Costa Adeje, is a popular marina area with a variety of restaurants and pubs. It's a terrific location to have a drink and take in the bustling scene while gazing out over the beautiful waterfront.

Tenerife's Santa Cruz:

Calle La Noria: This Santa Cruz de Tenerife street is well-known for its fashionable bars and pleasant taverns. It has a more casual and laid-back vibe, making it ideal for cocktails, artisan brews, or a glass of local wine.

Plaza de Espaa: Santa Cruz's main plaza, Plaza de Espaa, is surrounded by restaurants and cafés where you can relax and have a drink. This area is very lively on weekends and holidays, with live music and outside seating.

Puerto de la Cruz (Puerto de la Cruz):

Avenida de Colón: A vibrant boulevard with a variety of clubs and pubs, Avenida de Colón is located in Puerto de la Cruz. This neighborhood has a combination of classic Canarian taverns and contemporary bars, making for a diversified nightlife experience.

Those from Los Cristianos:

Avenida de Suecia: Avenida de Suecia is a boulevard in Los Cristianos that is dotted with clubs and taverns that serve to both residents and visitors. This section has a more relaxed and informal atmosphere, which is ideal for drinking and mingling.

Venues for Music and Entertainment:

Tramps: Tramps is a well-known nightclub in Playa de las Américas that offers international DJs and live music acts. It features a variety of music styles, including house, techno, and R&B.

The Hard Rock Café, located in Playa de las Américas, is a famous establishment that blends cuisine, beverages, and live music. It often welcomes local and foreign musicians as well as tribute acts, creating a vibrant scene for music fans.

Pirámide de Arona: In Playa de las Américas, this famous pyramid-shaped venue holds a variety of activities, including music concerts, comedy acts, and flamenco performances. It provides a one-of-a-kind and remarkable entertainment experience.

It is essential to drink responsibly, respect local traditions, and be careful of your surroundings while enjoying Tenerife's nightlife. Remember to dress correctly for the location you want to attend, since certain institutions may have dress rules.

Tenerife's dynamic bar and nightclub culture has something for everyone, whether you love dancing until the early hours or relaxing with friends over a drink in the evening. Explore the island's many locations, soak up the vibrant atmosphere, and make great experiences in Tenerife's nightlife.

Performances and Live Music

Tenerife has a thriving live music and performance culture, with several venues exhibiting outstanding performers and engaging shows. Whether you like live bands, classical music, or cultural programs, the island offers something to suit your musical preferences. Here's how to see live music and shows in Tenerife:

Auditorio de Tenerife (Santa Cruz de Tenerife): As an architectural marvel, the Auditorio de Tenerife is not only an aesthetic treat but also a cultural powerhouse. This historic theatre accommodates a variety of acts such as classical music concerts, opera, ballet, and theatrical shows. Tenerife Symphony Orchestra performs there, and it draws prominent national and worldwide musicians.

Clubs for Jazz and Blues:

Café Teatro Rayuela (Santa Cruz de Tenerife): This quaint café-theater in Santa Cruz presents frequent jazz and blues concerts, providing a warm and laid-back environment for music lovers.

Magma Arte y Congresos (Costa Adeje): Magma Arte y Congresos is a multi-purpose facility that offers jazz and blues events on occasion. Keep an eye out for forthcoming performances on their events calendar.

Pubs and bars:

Harley's American Restaurant & pub (Los Cristianos): This renowned Los Cristianos American-style pub has live music performances by rock, blues, and tribute bands. In a vibrant setting, enjoy wonderful cuisine, beverages, and entertaining acts.

Molly Malone's (Playa de las Américas): Known for its Irish bar ambience, Molly Malone's features live music sessions that include traditional Irish music as well as current covers. In this pleasant tavern, sit back, relax, and enjoy the vibrant melodies.

Festivals & Events of Cultural Interest

International Music Festival of the Canary Islands: The International Music Festival of the Canary Islands is a prominent event conducted yearly in various venues around Tenerife. It features famous orchestras, singers, and groups performing a wide spectrum of classical music.

Festival de las Artes del Sur (FAS): FAS is a yearly arts festival that highlights a variety of art genres such as music, theater, dance, and visual arts. It includes performances by local and international musicians at various venues across the island.

Beach Clubs and Outdoor Concerts

Hard Rock Hotel Beach Club (Playa Paraiso): This beachside facility presents open-air concerts and DJ performances, offering a one-of-a-kind musical experience by the sea. Look at their calendar for future events and performances.

Amarilla Golf & Country Club (Golf del Sur): This golf resort hosts outdoor concerts and live music events on occasion, showcasing a variety of genres from local and worldwide musicians.

When arranging to attend a live music performance, check event listings, venue websites, or local event guides for the most up-to-date schedules and ticket availability.

Tenerife's live music and performance culture combines traditional, modern, and worldwide influences, enabling you to immerse yourself in a melodious trip. Embrace the mesmerizing rhythms, discover the rich cultural legacy, and create lasting memories with Tenerife's wonderful live music and shows.

Gaming and Casinos

Tenerife has a thriving gambling sector, with multiple casinos where guests can enjoy an exciting night of entertainment and try their luck at a variety of games. Whether you're a seasoned gambler or seeking for an exciting encounter, the island has solutions to suit your gaming needs. Here's a guide to Tenerife's casinos and gaming:

Casino Playa de las Américas: One of the biggest and most popular casinos on the island, Casino Playa de las Américas is located in the middle of Playa de las Américas. It has a large variety of gambling alternatives, including as slot machines, roulette, blackjack, and poker. To improve the whole experience, the casino has a classy ambience, live music, and frequent events.

Casino Santa Cruz: Located in Santa Cruz de Tenerife's main city, Casino Santa Cruz offers an exquisite and polished gaming atmosphere. Table games, slot machines, and poker tournaments are all available at the casino. It also holds live concerts and events on occasion, which adds to the entertainment value.

Casino Taoro: Located in Puerto de la Cruz, Casino Taoro provides a one-of-a-kind gaming experience in a historic structure surrounded by lush gardens. The casino offers a variety of table games, including blackjack and roulette, as well as slot machines. Visitors may relax in an attractive setting while trying their luck at the gaming tables.

Casino Puerto de la Cruz: This casino, located in the famous tourist town of Puerto de la Cruz, offers a vibrant and exciting gaming experience. It has a variety of slot machines as well as table games such as blackjack and poker. The casino regularly provides live music and entertainment events, providing tourists with a lively environment.

Online gambling: If you prefer the ease of online gambling, there are many trustworthy online casinos that serve Tenerife residents. These platforms include a diverse range of casino games, including slots, roulette, blackjack, and live dealer games, all of which can be accessed from the comfort of your own home.

When visiting a casino in Tenerife, it is important to follow the dress code, which is often sophisticated casual. Guests must be at least 18 years old to enter most casinos, and identification may be required.

Please bet sensibly and minimize your gaming activity. Remember that gambling should be seen as enjoyment, and that you should always play within your means.

For those looking for a thrilling night out, Tenerife's casinos provide an exhilarating and elegant environment. Whether you're a newbie or a seasoned player, the casinos in Tenerife provide a variety of gaming alternatives and the opportunity to experience the excitement of gambling while also enjoying the island's dynamic entertainment scene.

CHAPTER 5: Practical Information

Safety and Travel Tips

Considerations for Health and Safety

Tenerife Health and Safety Considerations: Your Well-Being is a Priority. When visiting Tenerife, it is important to prioritize your health and safety in order to have a pleasant and memorable experience. Here are some important things to remember:

Travel Insurance: Make sure you have adequate travel insurance that covers medical bills, emergency evacuation, and other unexpected scenarios before you go. Familiarize yourself with the policy's coverage and maintain a copy of the insurance information on hand.

Tenerife offers well-equipped medical facilities, such as hospitals, clinics, and pharmacies. Seek medical attention at one of these places if you have any health problems. Carry a list of emergency contact numbers with you, including your insurance provider and local emergency services.

Drugs & Prescriptions: If you need prescription drugs, make sure you bring enough for your whole stay in Tenerife. Keep them in their original box and a copy of the prescription with you. It's also a good idea to have a small first-aid kit on hand with basic supplies for minor accidents or illnesses.

Sun protection: Although Tenerife has a lovely climate, the sun may be fierce. Wear sunscreen with a high SPF, sunglasses, and a hat to protect yourself from sunburn and heat-related diseases. Drink lots of water throughout the day, particularly during outdoor activities, to stay hydrated.

Water Safety: Follow safety recommendations and pay attention to warning flags on beaches while swimming or participating in water sports. Keep to specified swimming areas and be wary of strong currents. It is best to swim in places where lifeguards are present and to follow their recommendations.

Food and Water Safety: Tenerife normally maintains strong food and water safety regulations. If you are concerned about the safety of tap water, it is best to eat at recognized restaurants and use bottled water. When handling and ingesting food, use excellent hygiene.

Tenerife is a pretty secure place, however it is vital to practice care and be aware of your surroundings. Safeguard your possessions, avoid secluded or poorly lighted places at night, and utilize licensed taxis or recognized transportation providers.

Tenerife's volcanic nature makes it prone to periodic volcanic activity and earthquakes. Keep up to date on current events and follow local authorities' recommendations in the event of volcanic or seismic activity.

In the event of an emergency, phone the local emergency number, 112, for quick help. This number may be used for medical emergencies, fire services, and police.

Before your journey, read travel advisories and official sources for up-to-date information on health and safety precautions particular to Tenerife. You can assure a safe and pleasurable vacation on the lovely island of Tenerife by remaining informed and taking the essential measures.

Customs and Local Laws

When visiting Tenerife, it is essential to get acquainted with the local laws and traditions in order to have a polite and pleasurable trip. Consider the following crucial points:

Tenerife's legal drinking age is 18 years old, and alcohol use is permitted. It is unlawful to buy alcohol for anybody under the age of 21. Please drink sensibly and monitor your alcohol intake to preserve your health and safety.

Possession, sale, or use of illicit narcotics is severely outlawed in Tenerife and may result in serious legal penalties. To prevent any legal complications during your stay, it's essential to respect and follow local drug regulations.

Tenerife has established smoking prohibitions in order to preserve public health. Smoking is not permitted in enclosed public venues such as restaurants, bars, or public transit. Smoking is normally permitted in specified outdoor places, although it is important to be considerate of others and to respect non-smoking zones.

While there are popular nudist beaches in Tenerife, public nudity is typically not allowed outside of these designated zones. It is essential to dress correctly and respect local traditions and cultural norms while visiting non-nudist beaches.

Respect for Religious places and traditions: Tenerife has many religious places and traditions. Dress modestly and follow any special rules or guidelines offered while attending churches, temples, or other religious facilities. Respect others' privacy and religious customs.

Tenerife has spectacular natural vistas and a rich ecology, making environmental conservation a priority. It is critical to protect the environment by avoiding polluting, destroying natural habitats, or upsetting animals. Hike on approved paths and observe any directions or rules for conserving the island's natural beauty.

Tenerife has a bustling nightlife scene, especially in tourist regions. However, it is important to be courteous to others, particularly late at night. To respect the tranquillity of local inhabitants, keep noise levels in residential areas to a minimum.

Photography and Privacy: Always ask for permission before photographing people, especially natives. It is critical to respect their privacy as well as their cultural sensitivity. Avoid photographing sensitive sites such as military bases or government buildings.

Driving restrictions: If you want to hire a car in Tenerife, get acquainted with the local driving rules and restrictions. Follow traffic laws, use seat belts, and avoid driving when intoxicated. Parking restrictions must also be followed in order to avoid fines or penalties.

Tenerife is recognized for its kind and pleasant population. People should be greeted with a smile and a courteous "Hola" or "Buenos da/tardes" (good morning/afternoon). When conversing with locals, it is customary to say "gracias" (thank you) and "por favor" (please).

Respecting Tenerife's local laws, traditions, and cultural standards will guarantee a pleasant and courteous experience while enjoying all the island has to offer. Remember to have an open mind, accept the local culture, and interact respectfully with the people.

Emergency Phone Numbers.

When visiting Tenerife, it is essential to have access to emergency contacts to protect your safety and well-being. Here are some crucial numbers and contacts to remember:

Dial 112 for a general emergency.

Any kind of emergency, including medical aid, fire services, and police response, may be handled by dialing 112. It is a toll-free line that is available 24 hours a day, seven days a week.

Emergencies in Medicine:

Dial 112 for an ambulance or medical assistance.

Tenerife has numerous hospitals that are ready to manage medical emergencies. Here are a few examples of big hospitals:

+34 (922) 678 000 Hospital Universitario de Canarias

Nuestra Seora de Candelaria University Hospital: +34 (922) 602 000

+34 (922) 626 000 Hospital Universitario Quirónsalud Tenerife

Security and police:

Dial 091 for the National Police (Polica Nacional).

Local Police (Polica Local): Contact your local police station.

Tourist Information:

+34 900 101 813 for Emergency Tourism Assistance

This hotline assists travellers in a variety of languages, giving support and counseling in the event of an emergency, such as lost papers, accidents, or other travel-related difficulties.

Embassies and Consulates:

It's a good idea to write down the contact information for your country's consulate or embassy in Spain. They may help with misplaced passports, legal concerns, and other diplomatic services.

Assistance on the Road:

Contact the roadside assistance service offered by your car rental company or insurance provider in the event of a breakdown or vehicle-related emergency. Keep their contact information handy.

Remember to save these emergency contacts on your phone or keep them in a convenient place throughout your visit to Tenerife. It's also a good idea to have a copy of your travel insurance information and any pertinent medical information on hand.

In the event of an emergency, attempt to offer as much information as possible about your location and the nature of the issue, and follow the directions of the emergency service operators.

You can assure a quick reaction and support during any unexpected events while visiting Tenerife by being prepared and having access to the required emergency contacts.

Medical Services and Travel Insurance.

It is important to have enough travel insurance coverage while visiting Tenerife to safeguard your well-being and give financial help in the event of unforeseen medical expenditures. Important information about travel insurance and medical services in Tenerife is provided below:

Travel Protection:

It is highly advised that you acquire comprehensive travel insurance before traveling to Tenerife. Check to check whether your coverage covers medical bills, emergency medical evacuation, trip cancellation or interruption, lost or stolen possessions, and other unforeseeable events.

Examine the insurance coverage thoroughly, including any exclusions or limits. Check that it covers your personal requirements and the activities you want to do while in Tenerife.

Always carry a copy of your insurance policy, including emergency contact information, with you. Make sure you understand how to file a claim if one is required.

Medical Services:

Tenerife offers well-equipped medical facilities such as hospitals, clinics, and pharmacies that provide high-quality healthcare.

Hospitals: There are various hospitals on the island that provide complete medical treatment. Among the noteworthy hospitals are:

Canarias University Hospital is located in San Cristóbal de La Laguna. Phone: +34 (922) 678 000

Universitario Nuestra Seora de Candelaria Hospital: Located in Santa Cruz de Tenerife. Phone: +34 (922) 602 000

The Bellevue Hotel is located in Puerto de la Cruz. Phone: +34 (922) 380 512

Clinics and Urgent Care facilities: Smaller clinics and urgent care facilities may also be found in different cities and tourist destinations.

Pharmacies: Pharmacies (farmacias) are widely available on the island. They provide over-the-counter and prescription pharmaceuticals, as well as healthcare advice. Look for the green cross that denotes a drugstore.

Medical Payments and Expenses:

If you need medical attention in Tenerife, be sure you have the necessary funds. Check with your travel insurance provider about the process for medical expenditure reimbursement.

In the event of a medical emergency, phone the local emergency number (112) for urgent help or proceed straight to the emergency room of the closest hospital.

Medications on Prescription:

If you need prescription drugs, make sure you have enough for the length of your stay. Keep them in their original box and a copy of the prescription with you.

If you need to refill your prescription while in Tenerife, go to a pharmacy and present them with your drug information. They will walk you through the steps.

While medical facilities in Tenerife maintain excellent standards, it is recommended that you obtain travel insurance that covers medical evacuation, particularly if you want to participate in high-risk activities such as extreme sports or adventure tourism.

You may have peace of mind knowing that your health and safety are safeguarded while on vacation in Tenerife provided you have suitable travel insurance and are informed of the accessible medical services.

Money and Tipping.

When it comes to managing money in Tenerife, it is important to understand the local currency, payment options, and tipping customs. Here are some crucial items to remember:

Currency:

Tenerife's official currency is the Euro (EUR). Make sure you have enough Euros for your costs throughout your stay. Airports, banks, and exchange offices provide currency exchange services.

Most places, including hotels, restaurants, and stores, accept credit and debit cards. Carry some cash with you for little transactions and businesses that may not take cards.

Payment Options:

Visa and Mastercard credit and debit cards are generally accepted in Tenerife. It is, nevertheless, advisable to have a backup card or alternate payment option in case of problems.

ATMs: There are ATMs located across the island that enable you to withdraw cash. Check with your bank about any overseas withdrawal costs, and let them know about your vacation intentions ahead of time.

Contactless Payments: Contactless payment methods, such as mobile payment applications or contactless cards, are becoming more popular in a variety of places.

Tipping Customs:

Tipping is not required in Tenerife, however it is appreciated for excellent service. As a token of gratitude, it is traditional to offer a little tip.

Restaurants: If you are pleased with the service, a tip of 5-10% of the entire cost is customary. Some restaurants may include a service fee (referred to as "servicio") in the bill, so double-check before adding an extra tip.

Cafés and bars: It is customary to leave tiny change or round up the cost as a tip. You may leave a little bigger tip if the service is great.

Taxi Drivers: Tipping taxi drivers is not required, however rounding up the fee as a sign of gratitude is usual practice.

Other Services: It is normal to provide a tip for other services such as hotel employees, tour guides, or spa treatments if you believe the service was outstanding.

Taxation and Price Transparency:

Taxes and service costs are usually included in Tenerife prices. Unless any extra costs are indicated individually, the listed amount is what you should expect to pay.

When dealing with money, remember to be courteous and thoughtful. To guarantee a nice and peaceful experience throughout your stay in Tenerife, it's vital to have a basic awareness of the local conventions and rules around tipping.

By being kind with your money and following local tipping customs, you can contribute to a good and polite exchange while enjoying Tenerife's services and hospitality.

Useful Phrases and Vocabulary

Basic Greetings and Expressions

Interacting with locals in Tenerife can be a delightful experience, and knowing some basic greetings and expressions will help you make a positive connection. Here are a few commonly used phrases to get you started:

Greetings:

Hello: Hola (oh-la)

Good morning: Buenos días (bway-nos dee-as)

Good afternoon: Buenas tardes (bway-nas tar-des)

Good evening: Buenas noches (bway-nas no-ches)

Polite Expressions:

Please: Por favor (por fa-vor)

Thank you: Gracias (gra-thi-as)

You're welcome: De nada (de na-da)

Excuse me: Perdón (per-don)

I'm sorry: Lo siento (lo see-en-to)

Introductions:

My name is...: Mi nombre es... (mee nom-bre es...)

What is your name?: ¿Cómo te llamas? (ko-mo te ya-mas?)

Nice to meet you: Mucho gusto (moo-cho goo-sto)\

Basic Conversational Phrases:

How are you?: ¿Cómo estás? (ko-mo es-tas?)

I'm good, thank you: Estoy bien, gracias (es-toy byen, gra-thi-as)

Yes: Sí (see)

No: No (no)

I don't understand: No entiendo (no en-tyen-do)

Could you please repeat that?: ¿Podrías repetir, por favor? (po-dree-as re-pe-teer, por fa-vor?)

Ordering Food and Drinks:

I would like...: Me gustaría... (me goos-ta-ree-a)

Can I have the menu, please?: ¿Puedo ver el menú, por favor? (pwe-do ver el me-noo, por fa-vor?)

Water: Agua (a-gwa)

Coffee: Café (ka-fe)

Beer: Cerveza (cer-ve-tha)

Cheers!: ¡Salud! (sa-lud)

Remember to greet people with a smile and use these phrases as a starting point to engage with locals. The people of Tenerife are warm and welcoming, and making an effort to communicate in their language will be appreciated.

While many locals speak English, especially in tourist areas, using a few basic Spanish phrases will go a long way in fostering positive connections and enhancing your cultural experience in Tenerife.

Numbers and Directions

Numbers and Directions in Tenerife: Navigating and Communicating Numerically

When exploring Tenerife, it's helpful to familiarize yourself with numbers and basic directions to navigate the island and communicate effectively. Here are some key phrases and expressions:

Numbers:

1 - One: Uno (oo-no)

2 - Two: Dos (doss)

3 - Three: Tres (tress)

4 - Four: Cuatro (kwa-tro)

5 - Five: Cinco (sink-o)

6 - Six: Seis (says)

7 - Seven: Siete (syet-te)

8 - Eight: Ocho (oh-cho)

9 - Nine: Nueve (nwe-ve)

10 - Ten: Diez (dyeth)

11 - Eleven: Once (on-se)

12 - Twelve: Doce (doh-se)

20 - Twenty: Veinte (vin-te)

30 - Thirty: Treinta (tre-in-ta)

50 - Fifty: Cincuenta (sink-wen-ta)

100 - One hundred: Cien (syen)

1000 - One thousand: Mil (meel)

Directions:

Where is...?: ¿Dónde está...? (don-de es-ta)

Right: Derecha (de-re-cha)

Left: Izquierda (eez-kee-er-da)

Straight ahead: Todo recto (to-do rek-to)

Turn: Girar (hee-rar)

Street: Calle (ka-yeh)

Avenue: Avenida (a-ve-nee-da)

Square: Plaza (pla-sa)

North: Norte (nor-te)

South: Sur (soor)

East: Este (es-te)

West: Oeste (oes-te)

Examples:

Where is the beach?: ¿Dónde está la playa? (don-de es-ta la pla-ya)

Turn right at the next intersection: Gira a la derecha en el próximo cruce (hee-ra a la de-re-cha en el pro-ksi-mo kroo-se)

The restaurant is on the left side of the street: El restaurante está a la izquierda de la calle (el res-tau-ran-te es-ta a la eez-kee-er-da de la ka-yeh)

These basic phrases and expressions will assist you in communicating numerical information and asking for directions while exploring Tenerife. Feel free to practice them and don't hesitate to ask locals for help if needed.

Dining and Shopping Phrases

Dining and Shopping Phrases in Tenerife: Enhancing Your Culinary and Retail Experiences

When dining at restaurants or shopping in Tenerife, knowing some basic phrases can enhance your experience and make interactions smoother. Here are some useful phrases to assist you:

Dining Phrases:

Can I have a table for [number of people], please?: ¿Puedo tener una mesa para [número de personas], por favor? (pwe-do te-ner oo-na me-sa pa-ra [nu-meh-ro de per-so-nas], por fa-vor?)

What do you recommend?: ¿Qué me recomienda? (keh me re-ko-myen-da?)

I would like to order...: Me gustaría pedir... (me goo-sta-ree-a pe-deer...)

What are the specials of the day?: ¿Cuáles son las especialidades del día? (kwa-les son las es-pe-thya-lee-da-des del dee-a?)

Can I have the bill, please?: ¿Me puede traer la cuenta, por favor? (me pwe-de tra-er la kwen-ta, por fa-vor?)

It was delicious: Estuvo delicioso (es-tu-vo de-li-thyo-so)

Do you have vegetarian/vegan options?: ¿Tienen opciones vegetarianas/veganas? (tye-nen op-syo-nes be-ge-ta-rya-nas/ve-ga-nas?)

Is service included?: ¿Está incluido el servicio? (es-ta in-kloo-ee-do el ser-vee-thyo?)

Shopping Phrases:

How much does it cost?: ¿Cuánto cuesta? (kwan-to kwe-sta?)

Do you have this in a different size/color?: ¿Lo tiene en otra talla/color? (lo tyeh-ne en o-tra ta-lya/ko-lor?)

Can I try this on?: ¿Puedo probármelo? (pwe-do pro-bar-meh-lo?)

Do you accept credit cards?: ¿Aceptan tarjetas de crédito? (a-cep-tan tar-he-tas de kre-di-to?)

Can I have a receipt, please?: ¿Me puede dar un recibo, por favor? (me pwe-de dar oon re-see-bo, por fa-vor?)

I'm just browsing: Solo estoy mirando (so-lo es-toy mee-ran-do)

Do you have any discounts or sales?: ¿Tienen algún descuento o rebajas? (tye-nen al-gun des-kwen-to o re-ba-has?)

I'm looking for...: Estoy buscando... (es-toy boo-skan-do...)

Remember to greet with a smile and use polite phrases like "please" (por favor) and "thank you" (gracias) during your interactions. Most people in Tenerife speak Spanish, but many also understand English, especially in tourist areas.

Engaging with locals using these phrases will not only make your dining and shopping experiences more enjoyable but also show your appreciation for the local culture and language.

CHAPTER 6: Exploring Tenerife.

15 Things to do and See in Tenerife

The Caldera

When touring Tenerife's La Caldera and the area that surrounds it, you'll encounter pine trees, volcanic terrain, and vistas upon views. La Caldera is a volcanic crater located in La Orotava Valley, which covers the northern section of the island's central coast. La Orotava has paths, including those surrounding La Caldera and its leisure area, in addition to beautiful views. The La Caldera crater, which is easily accessible, has picnic tables and a playground, as well as other amenities like as a café. However, you may be more interested in exploring the woods paradise that surrounds all of this, notably the loop that encircle the crater and wanders out into the mountainous scenery beyond. The 3-hour journey, which starts in the recreation area, goes through the region's mossy, fern-filled landscape and provides spectacular views of Tenerife, especially El Teide.

Tenerife Auditorium (Tenerife Auditorium)

Tenerife Auditorium is one of the capital's most distinctive buildings, with its wave-like profile and contemporary design dominating over the coastline of Santa Cruz port. The sculptural masterpiece also serves as a prominent entertainment facility, hosting concerts, operas, and dance events.

Tenerife Immaculate Conception Church

The Tenerife Church of the Immaculate Conception, built in 1498, is Tenerife's oldest church and one of Santa Cruz' most renowned structures. According to legend, the initial church was built on the orders of Alonso Fernandez de Lugo, leader of the Spanish invaders, making it an important location in the city's creation.

Teide National Park (Parque Nacional del Teide)

Teide National Park (Parque Nacional del Teide), the biggest and oldest national park in the Canary Islands, is one of Tenerife's major attractions. Mount Teide, Spain's tallest mountain, is located here. The park's rough scenery, a UNESCO World Heritage Site, is breathtaking—a geological marvel with an expanse of jagged lava fields, ancient calderas, and volcanic peaks.

The Masca Valley

The untamed landscapes of Tenerife's Masca Valley are among the most spectacular, with rocky cliffs, wooded pathways, and waterfalls. The secluded canyon provides an exciting setting for a trek, with the route winding down into the valley and ending at a black-sand beach.

El Teide (Mount Teide)

Mt. Teide (El Teide) is the highest peak in the Canary Islands and Spain, rising 12,198 feet (3,718 meters) above sea level. Visitors to Tenerife may stand atop a volcano and see out across other islands such as La Palma and Gran Canaria if the clouds cooperate, whether they arrive by foot or by cable car.

Bodegas Monje (Monje Winery)

Discover the Canary Islands' viniculture heritage at the Monje Winery (Bodegas Monje) in Tenerife's picturesque La Hollera. Taste the reds, whites, and rosés; stroll the vineyards; and see how ancient techniques and new innovation collide. Then, from the on-site restaurant's patio, take in some of the greatest views on the island.

The Roques of Garca

Los Roques de Garca, a collection of oddly sculpted rocks in the shadow of Tenerife's famously explosive Teide volcano, is one of the main attractions of the UNESCO-listed Teide National Park.

The pyroclastic rocks, formed by years of past volcanic activity, are most renowned for their towering size and unusual formations, with some seeming to defy gravity and others taking on an otherworldly appearance. The most renowned rocks are the 'Roque Cinchado,' also known as 'God's Finger,' which has become one of Tenerife's most distinctive monuments, and the towering La Catedral, the highest at 200 meters and a popular climbing challenge. Each rock has a unique name, such as 'El Queso,' 'Roques Blancos,' and 'Torrotito,' and the best way to see them all is to trek the 2 hour round trip around the valley.

Valley of La Orotava

La Orotava Valley has some of Tenerife's most beautiful scenery. This gorgeous valley stretches from the Teide Volcano and is filled with vineyards, banana plantations, and pine-clad slopes renowned for trekking. The old village of La Orotava provides as a base for valley adventures.

Vilaflor

Vilaflor, Tenerife's highest settlement, is perched on a rocky plateau at 1,400m and is surrounded by pine-covered mountains, craggy lava plains, and wildflower meadows. Vilaflor, located in the Teide National Park's foothills, is a popular starting place for hiking and climbing trips, as well as being known for its local wineries and vineyards.The Paisaje Lunar (lunar landscape), an otherworldly lava valley with strange rock formations formed out of stunning white tuff, is a regional attraction. Nearby attractions include the Fuente Altam thermal springs, the Sanctuary of Santo Hermano Pedro, and El Pino Gordo (the Fat Pine), the biggest tree in the Canary Islands.

Drago Park (Parque del Drago)

Drago Park (Parque del Drago) in Icod de los Vinos, Tenerife, is known for its 800-year-old Dragon Tree, which is the oldest of its type in the Canary Islands. It's best seen from inside the botanical garden, which also has a large variety of indigenous animals, birds, caverns, and observation platforms.

Teleférico del Teide (Teide Cable Car)

More than merely admiring Spain's tallest volcano from afar, take the Teide Cable Car (Teleférico del Teide) to the summit. This smooth journey will take you to the peak of Mount Tiede, where you can go on walks through the exotic vistas of UNESCO-listed Teide National Park or stargaze from Teide Observatory.

The Médano

El Médano's sweeping coastline breezes and long sandy beaches provide some of the greatest windsurfing and kitesurfing conditions on Tenerife. The ancient Spanish village, perched along the southeast coast, provides a laid-back alternative to the island's biggest beach resorts, making it a popular destination for both families and adrenaline seekers.

Playa de las Vistas (Las Vistas Beach)

Many beaches beckon on Tenerife, but there's a reason Las Vistas' broad expanse of golden sand is one of the island's most popular. There is something for everyone with a variety of amenities and vivid blue umbrellas and beach chairs. The seas right off the beach separate into two coves that are very calm and suitable for swimming. There are also several bars, restaurants, and retail opportunities both on and near the beach. Water sports, beach volleyball, and other recreational activities are popular here as well. Because the beach is well-known, it might be crowded with other visitors, especially during the summer months. The beach is a fantastic alternative for people vacationing with children because of its accessibility and relative safety. Those looking for more daring activities may go boating or scuba diving in the seas off the shore, which are often launched from the beach.

Jungle Park Las Guilas

Tenerife's Las Guilas Jungle Park is a treasure trove of rare birds, big cats, lemurs, monkeys, penguins, reptiles, and other animals. Explore the park, marvel at the daily flying and feeding exhibits, go on toboggan slopes, and then refuel at the onsite food restaurants.

Tips for Solo Travelers to Tenerife

Tenerife is an excellent choice for lone visitors. It's a lovely island with a lot to offer, from breathtaking landscape to a thriving nightlife. Here are some suggestions for solitary visitors visiting Tenerife:

- Consider staying at a hostel or guesthouse. This is an excellent method to meet and make friends with other solo travelers. Tenerife has a plethora of hostels and guesthouses that appeal to lone visitors.
- Participate in a tour or activity group. This is yet another excellent approach to meet new people and establish new friends. There are several tour companies and activity

providers in Tenerife that specialize in tours and activities for single travelers.

- You are free to explore the island on your own. There's no need to feel obligated to be around other people all of the time. Tenerife is an excellent destination for independent exploration. Hiking, swimming, and visiting museums are just a few of the activities available.
- Keep an eye on your surroundings. As with any other tourist location, stay alert of your surroundings and take measures against petty theft. Tenerife, on the other hand, is a usually safe place for lone travelers.
- Relax and have a good time! Tenerife is a lovely island with much to offer. Soak in the sun, swim in the sea, and see all the island has to offer.

Tips for Female Solo Travelers to Tenerife

- Keep to a secure zone. When picking your lodging, be sure you stay in a secure neighborhood. This entails remaining in a well-lit location with a high population density.
- Keep an eye on your surroundings. Tenerife, like any other holiday location, requires you to be alert of your

surroundings. This entails being aware of who is around you and where you are going.

- Believe your intuition. If something does not feel right, it most likely is not. Don't be scared to leave if you're uncomfortable in a scenario.
- Take preventative measures against petty theft. In certain areas of Tenerife, petty thievery is a concern. Keep your belongings near to you and don't leave them unattended to protect yourself.
- Don't be hesitant to seek assistance. If you want assistance, do not be hesitant to request it. Tenerife's residents are typically quite pleasant and helpful.
- Carry a whistle or personal alarm with you. This may be an excellent method of discouraging prospective attackers.
- Learn some fundamental Spanish phrases. This will help you converse with locals and navigate the city.
- Keep in touch with relatives and friends back home. Tell them where you're going and when you expect to return.
- Bring a self-defense item with you. This might range from pepper spray to a personal alarm.
- Be mindful of your drinking. Drink in moderation, particularly if you're alone. This increases your vulnerability to assault.

Tips for Family Travelers to Tenerife

- Choose a resort that is suitable for families. There are several family-friendly resorts in Tenerife, so select one with activities and facilities that your family will like.
- Go to the water parks. Tenerife is home to some of the world's top water parks, including Siam Park and Aqualand. These parks can keep your family occupied for hours on end.
- Hike or ride your bike. Tenerife boasts several hiking and bike paths that are ideal for families. These paths provide breathtaking views of the island and are an excellent way to get some exercise.
- Pay a visit to Loro Parque. Loro Parque is a world-renowned zoo and aquarium with around 4,000 species. This is an excellent resource for learning about animals from throughout the globe.
- Visit a whale watching site. Tenerife is an excellent location for whale viewing. Whales and dolphins may often be seen swimming off the island's shore.

- Explore the Teide National Park. Teide National Park is a **UNESCO** World Heritage Site and home to Mount Teide, Spain's highest peak. This is an excellent location for hiking, stargazing, and exploration.

- Spend some time on the beach. Tenerife offers some of the world's greatest beaches. Soak in the rays, swim in the sea, and make sandcastles.

Top Booking Resources:

When it comes to travel, I have a few go-to firms that regularly provide fantastic discounts, good customer service, and tremendous value. These are my favourite options, and they are always the first places I go when looking for travel plans. Here are some of my favorite booking resources:

Skyscanner - Skyscanner is my preferred flight search engine.. It searches tiny websites and low-cost airlines that other search engines often neglect. It is certainly the best place to start your flight search.

Hostelworld - The greatest resource for hostel lodgings is Hostelworld. It has the greatest inventory, the most user-friendly search interface, and the most hostels available globally.

Booking.com - When it comes to general booking, Booking.com regularly provides the best and lowest prices. They feature a large assortment of low-cost lodgings. They consistently supplied the most reasonable pricing across all booking websites in all of my testing.

Get Your Guide is a fantastic online marketplace for tours and excursions. They provide a plethora of tour alternatives in cities all over the globe, ranging from culinary workshops and walking tours to street art lessons and much more!

SafetyWing specializes in delivering simple and cheap insurance coverage for digital nomads and long-term travelers. Their monthly plans are competitively priced, and they provide great customer service and an easy-to-use claims procedure, making it a perfect solution for individuals who are always on the go.

LifeStraw - My go-to business for reusable water bottles with built-in filters is LifeStraw. You can always be confident that your drinking water is pure and safe with their products, no matter where you are.

Unbound Merino - Unbound Merino is an excellent option for lightweight, durable, and easy-to-clean travel clothes. Their attire is made with travelers in mind, providing comfort and utility.

These booking services have constantly shown to be dependable and effective, offering passengers the greatest alternatives for flights, lodgings, excursions, insurance, and travel necessities. Use these services to make your journey planning easier and more fun.

Conclusion

Finally, our thorough Tenerife travel guide has offered essential information and insights for first-time visitors to this lovely island. Tenerife provides a broad choice of activities for tourists to enjoy, from its gorgeous terrain and agreeable temperature to its rich culture and hospitable residents.

We investigated the island's topography, climate, culture, and language, offering a strong basis for better understanding and appreciating Tenerife's distinctive characteristics. Dos and don'ts were supplied to guarantee appropriate conduct, while information on traveling to Tenerife, visa requirements, and lodging possibilities gave practical advice for organizing a successful vacation.

The book also delves into the gastronomic culture of the island, covering traditional Canarian foods, prominent restaurants and cafés, street food, and local markets. Dietary restrictions and particular needs were given great consideration, guaranteeing that all passengers may find adequate alternatives to excite their taste senses.

Furthermore, the book shed light on Tenerife's thriving nightlife, which includes pubs, nightclubs, live music, and shows, providing possibilities to immerse oneself in the island's lively entertainment scene.

Health and safety precautions, emergency contacts, travel insurance, and medical facilities were all fully discussed, stressing the need of prioritizing well-being throughout the trip. Money, tipping etiquette, basic greetings, numbers, directions, eating words, and shopping phrases were all offered to assist successful communication and improve the entire experience while engaging with locals.

Tenerife, with its breathtaking scenery, cultural riches, and friendly welcome, guarantees tourists an amazing experience. By following the advice and insights offered in this book, travelers will be well-prepared to begin on their Tenerife trip, assuring a seamless and delightful encounter.

So pack your bags, immerse yourself in Tenerife's beauty, and make lifetime memories on this wonderful Canary Island.

Printed in Great Britain
by Amazon